201

Positive Psychology Applications

201

Positive Psychology Applications

Promoting Well-Being in Individuals and Communities

FREDRIKE BANNINK

W.W. Norton & Company
Independent Publishers Since 1923
New York | London

Copyright © 2017 by Fredrike Bannink

All rights reserved
Printed in the United States of America
First Edition

For information about permission to reproduce selections from this book,
write to Permissions, W. W. Norton & Company, Inc.,
500 Fifth Avenue, New York, NY 10110

For information about special discounts for bulk purchases, please contact
W. W. Norton Special Sales at specialsales@wwnorton.com or 800-233-4830

Manufacturing by Edwards Brothers Malloy
Production manager: Christine Critelli

ISBN 978-0-393-71220-9

W. W. Norton & Company, Inc.
500 Fifth Avenue, New York, N.Y. 10110
www.wwnorton.com

W. W. Norton & Company Ltd.
15 Carlisle Street, London W1D 3BS

1 2 3 4 5 6 7 8 9 0

Contents

Acknowledgments vii

Introduction: From What's Wrong to What's Strong ix

1 Positive Psychology 1

2 Positive Emotion 38

3 Engagement 78

4 Relationships 118

5 Meaning 152

6 Accomplishment 194

7 Further Applications 225

Applications at a Glance 241
References 251
Websites 273
Index 277
About the Author 303

Acknowledgments

In and of themselves, differences are just differences. But some people (and animals) make a difference that makes a difference in my life and my work. In one way or the other, they all assisted me in writing this book.

It goes without saying that I very much appreciate the contributions of my colleagues, students, and above all my clients, who have helped me discover, apply, and improve my work over the years.

I thank Deborah Malmud for publishing the English translation (this book was originally written in Dutch) and everyone else who devoted their time and energy to making this book a reality.

To my husband, I am grateful for your continuing love and support. To my four Italian cats, mille grazie for keeping me company during the many pleasant hours of writing.

Introduction

From What's Wrong to What's Strong

Positive psychology is a rapidly growing movement in psychology, focusing on well-being and optimal functioning. This orientation offers new possibilities in (mental) health, education, the workplace, journalism, technology, sports, and society. Positive psychology (PP) focuses on strengthening capabilities to lead a pleasant, good, and meaningful life, with positive relationships and accomplishment.

Until recently, the general focus was on what is wrong with individuals and communities. Nowadays, we are starting to see a better balance between the focus on what is wrong—weaknesses and limitations—and what is right—strengths and possibilities: *from what's wrong to what's strong*.

Looking at (mental) health, we came to understand that health is not the same as the absence of illness. It concerns the absence of (psycho) pathology *and* the presence of well-being. Psychotherapy should therefore no longer be the place where the focus is solely on repairing problems, but also the place where strengths are discovered and used, positive emotions are amplified, and hope, gratitude, and optimism are nourished.

Research shows that psychopathology and positive mental health are two different but complementary indicators of mental health (Keyes, 2005). Their relationship is a negative one: Psychological problems are more often found in people with poor mental health than in people with good mental health. But the relationship is limited: The degree of psychopathology does not say much about the degree of positive mental health, and vice versa. Someone may experience well-being in combination with psychological symptoms, and the absence of mental illness does not guarantee high levels of well-being.

Meanwhile, PP produced a large number of studies of the constructs (also called "family members") in the domain of PP, such as optimism, well-being, gratitude, resilience, flow, hope, courage, and positive emotions. However, their results should be interpreted with some caution. PP is a relatively new science, and although its applications can be effective in promoting well-being, the quality of the research is variable. A sufficient number of well-designed randomized controlled studies have not yet been administered; in the area of research and methodology, there is still much room for improvement. Another key focus is on how to motivate people to implement PP applications and keep them involved in (re)using them. This is also true—perhaps to an even greater degree—for traditional problem-focused applications.

More and more professionals are discovering the potential of PP, and lately many books on PP have been published. A book that presents all the applications—besides theory and research—was lacking until now. This book is written for all professionals working with individuals and communities who want to focus (more) on strengths and what is working. This book may be useful as a self-help tool also.

The chapter structure is based on the five pillars of the *well-being theory* of Seligman, one of the founders of PP. This leading model identifies five essential elements of well-being. The introductory chapter on PP is followed by a description of the research and the many applications in the fields of these five elements: positive emotion, engagement, relationships, meaning, and accomplishment (PERMA). The final chapter discusses questionnaires, cards, (online) games, and the possibilities of e-health and m-health.

Arranging the applications within the five pillars is my personal choice and feels obvious, although some applications may be placed under a different pillar. Furthermore, "one size fits all" is not applicable here; each application should be carefully tailored to the person(s) and the context.

The many PP applications are complemented by a number of solution-focused applications that show some similarities with PP (Bannink & Jackson, 2011); both veer away from pathology and share a focus on what is going right. The focus of PP is on strengths, while solution-focused interviewing (Bannink, 2010a) focuses on what works.

In this book, you will find 200 applications, taking the "what" to the "how." I do not pretend to have addressed all of them, but most applications are included. At the end of the book, you will find all applications at a glance. You may present them to your clients, students, employees, or coachees or use them yourself. Most of them can be used in several settings, although I use the term *clients* in all applications. Stories and cases are added to give you the opportunity to integrate the theory and applications.

With this book, I hope to invite you to apply PP (more often) to discover and promote the best in individuals and communities.

—Fredrike Bannink

201

Positive Psychology Applications

Promoting Well-Being in Individuals and Communities

1

Positive Psychology

*Positive psychology does not have to be constructed from the ground up.
It merely involves a change of focus from repairing what is worst in life to
creating what is best.*

—MARTIN SELIGMAN

This chapter offers a description of positive psychology (PP) and its short history. Seligman's *well-being theory* is presented, the five elements of which serve as the basis for this book: positive emotion, engagement, relationships, meaning, and accomplishment (PERMA). The classification of *character strengths* is explored, and subsequently the areas of PP are described. These areas are, besides psychotherapy and psychiatry, the workplace, education, technology, journalism, sports, and society. The underlying message of PP is that life for everyone can be better if certain conditions are met (Wong, Wong, McDonald, & Klaassen, 2007).

Positive Psychology

PP is the scientific and social movement in psychology in which well-being and optimal functioning (individual, relational, organizational, and societal) are the main focus. In the area of mental health, Keyes and Lopez (2005) stated that mental health is not the same as the absence of mental illness. Mental health is more; it is the presence of well-being. It is not just about "what's wrong with you," but also about "what's right with you."

The World Health Organization (WHO; 2005) described mental health as a state of well-being in which the individual effectuates his or her capabilities and is able to cope with the normal stresses of life, is productive in work, and contributes to society. The founders of PP, Seligman and Csikszentmihalyi (2000, p. 7), argued that psychology can cover a much wider area than just (mental) health: "Psychology is not just a health science concerned with illness: it could be larger. It is about work, education, insight, love, growth, and play." There are several definitions of PP, which differ slightly:

- PP is the scientific study of human strengths and virtues (Sheldon & King, 2001).
- PP is the study of what constitutes the pleasant life, the engaged life, and the meaningful life (Seligman, 2002).
- PP is the study of the conditions and processes that contribute to the flourishing or optimal functioning of people, groups, and institutions (Gable & Haidt, 2005).
- PP studies what makes life most worth living (Peterson, 2006a, 2006b).

To summarize: PP is the scientific study of human flourishing and an applied approach to optimal functioning. It has also been defined as the study of the strengths and virtues that enable individuals, communities and organizations to thrive.

A Short History

Seligman likes to tell the following story about how his daughter Nikki changed his life and work:

> The notion of a positive psychology movement began at a moment in time a few months after I had been elected president of the American Psychological Association. It took place in my garden while I was weeding with my 5-year-old daughter, Nikki. I have to confess that even though I write books about children, I'm really not all that good with them. I am goal-oriented and time-urgent, and when I am weeding in the garden, I am actually trying to get the weeding done. Nikki, however, was throwing weeds into the air and dancing around. I yelled at her. She walked away, came back, and said, "Daddy, I want to talk to you." "Yes, Nikki?" "Daddy, do you remember before my fifth birthday? From the time I was three to the time I was five I was a whiner. I whined every day. When I turned five, I decided not to whine anymore. That was the hardest thing I've ever done. And if I can stop whining, you can stop being such a grouch." (Seligman, 2005, p. 3).

This was an eye-opener for Seligman. He realized that Nikki was right; for fifty years he had often been cranky for no good reason. He realized that raising children was about identifiying and nurturing their strongest qualities, what they own and are best at, and helping them find niches in which they can best live out these positive qualities. The *Nikki principle* was born.

The Nikki principle turned out to be important not only to Seligman personally and for the education of his daughter, but also for the whole of psychology: PP became the orientation emanating from the strengths of people and the assumption that happiness not only is the result of the right genes or chance, but also is found by identifying and using the strengths that someone possesses.

PP was in the spotlight when Seligman (known for researching *learned helplessness*) became president of the American Psychological Association in 1998. It was his mission to put PP on the map. Seligman, Steen, Park, and Peterson (2005) stated that it is not the intention of PP to replace all that is known about human suffering and disease, but rather to supplement it and to achieve a better balance in understanding what people go through: the highs and lows in life and everything in between.

> The message of the positive psychology movement is to remind our field that it has been deformed. Psychology is not just the study of disease, weakness, and damage; it also is the study of strength and virtue. Treatment is not just fixing what is wrong; it also is building what is right. And in this quest for what is best, Positive

Psychology does not rely on wishful thinking, self-deception or hand-waving; instead it tries to adapt what is best in the scientific method to the unique problems that human behavior presents in all its complexity. (p. 4)

THE GRANT STUDY

The focus on (mental) health did not start with Seligman and his daughter Nikki. Already in 1937, the entrepreneur and philanthropist William T. Grant had, along with the director of Harvard University Health Service, noted that medical research was focused on diseases too much. They saw that few scientists thought it appropriate to investigate people who felt good and were doing well. For this reason, they selected for an intensive medical and psychological examination a sample of healthy individuals from several consecutive school years (268 persons between 1939 and 1944 studying at Harvard), and the "Grant Study" was born (Vaillant, 2002; see Chapter 4). This is the longest longitudinal study ever done on the development of adults. From adolescence to late in life—for seventy-five years—these men were followed to discover how people can grow old healthily.

Well-Being

Seligman (2011) based his *well-being theory* on five pillars. He added the third and fifth pillars to his earlier happiness theory. The acronym for the five pillars (or elements) is PERMA: positive emotion, engagement, relationships, meaning, and accomplishment. Each element itself has three properties:

1. It contributes to well-being.
2. Many people pursue it for its own sake, not merely to get any of the other elements.
3. It is defined and measured independently of the other elements.

These five elements can help people reach a life of fulfillment, happiness, and meaning. The model can also be applied to institutions to develop programs to help people develop new cognitive and emotional tools. The five elements are:

1. **Positive emotion:** Focusing on positive emotions is more than just smiling; it is the ability to be optimistic and view the past, present, and future in a positive perspective. This positive view in life, where there is room for fun and enjoyment, can help us in relationships and work and inspire us to be more creative and take more chances. It is about experiencing positive emotions: To what extent do we feel happy and content?

2. **Engagement:** Finding activities that take our full engagement helps us to learn, grow, and nurture personal happiness. This life of involvement refers to our commitment to do what we do: To what extent do we experience a sense of personal fulfillment?

3. **Relationships:** Having relationships and social connections is one of the most important aspects of life. We are social animals that thrive on connection, love, intimacy, and a strong emotional and physical interaction with other humans. Building positive relationships with our parents, siblings, peers, and friends is important for spreading love and joy. Having strong relationships gives us support in difficult times.

4. **Meaning:** Finding meaning and a reason why we are on this earth is important to living a life of happiness and fulfillment. Rather than the pursuit of pleasure and material wealth there is an actual purpose for our life. To understand the greater impact of our work and why we chose to pursuit that work will help us enjoy our tasks more and become more satisfied and happier. Living a meaningful life is not only about us, but also about something larger than us—about altruism and caring for others: To what extent do we have the feeling of being part of and contributing to a greater whole?

5. **Accomplishment:** Having goals and ambition in life is also important. We should make realistic goals that can be met; just putting in the effort to achieve those goals can already give us a sense of satisfaction. When we finally achieve those goals, we will experience a sense of pride and fulfillment. Pursuing success, accomplishment, winning, achievement, and mastery for their own sake will help us thrive and flourish.

The *PERMA-Profiler* measures these five pillars, along with negative emotion and health (Butler & Kern, 2015).

In accordance with the aforementioned WHO definition of positive mental health, well-being may be divided into three components: *emotional, psychological, and social well-being* (Westerhof & Keyes, 2008).

- *Emotional well-being* is satisfaction with life and experiencing positive feelings such as happiness and interest. This is also known as subjective well-being (Diener, Suh, Lucas, & Smith, 1999).
- *Psychological well-being* focuses on optimal functioning in individuals. Self-realization is central, including the idea of purpose and direction in life, the idea of development, and a positive attitude toward yourself (Ryff, 1989).
- *Social well-being* focuses on optimal functioning in social groups and society. This includes the idea of being part of a community, the idea that others appreciate your activities, and a positive attitude toward those around you (Keyes, 1998).

Discussion is ongoing about the precise relationship between these three components of positive mental health.

Character Strengths

The starting point of PP is that mainstream psychology is biased toward weaknesses and not toward strengths. PP focuses not only on repairing what is wrong—weaknesses, errors, problems, and limitations—but also on building what is right—strengths, solutions, capabilities, and possibilities. An approach that uses character strengths provides opportunities for individual and professional development. It assumes that a focus on achievement, personal qualities, and character strengths will allow for change. Linley, Nielsen, Gillett, and Biswas-Diener (2010) found that people who use their charater strengths score higher on self-confidence (Wood, Linley, Maltby, Kashdan, & Hurling, 2011), on perceived competence (Proctor, Maltby, & Linley, 2011), on the realization of goals (Linley et al., 2010), and on well-being (Linley et al., 2010). Moreover, character strengths act as a buffer against mental disorders (Seligman & Csikszentmihalyi, 2000). For example, optimism prevents the occurrence of depression.

The good news about character strengths is that they can be discovered, acquired, practiced, and further developed and that everyone has them, although their configuration differs per person. Moreover, all character strengths are positive, and they can strengthen each other and compensate one another. This approach also ensures that motivation is increased, because people work on the basis of what they are good at. Growth is promoted, because people look at possibilities instead of impossibilities.

Sheldon, Jose, Kashdan, and Jarden (2015) compiled a list of ten key character strengths associated with achieving goals and well-being:

1. Curiosity
2. The sense of control over good and bad events
3. Meaning in life

4. Grit (perseverance)
5. Gratitude
6. Use of strengths and knowledge
7. Orientation toward happiness: pleasure
8. Orientation toward happiness: engagement
9. Orientation toward happiness: meaning
10. Savoring

According to their research, the two most important are grit and curiosity. People need grit to achieve long-term goals (see Chapter 6), and people need curiosity to experience greater well-being: If you work in areas where new things can be discovered, you will feel happier.

When looking for and building character strengths, usually one looks to one strength instead of how multiple strengths are interrelated and may reinforce each other. However, combining two character strengths may, for example, further reduce the risk of suicide. Kleiman, Adams, Kashdan, and Riskind (2013) found that adults who barely have suicidal thoughts are grateful (see Chapter 5) and have grit (see Chapter 6). This has to do with the fact that gratitude is related to giving attention to the outside world (feeling the cool breeze as you walk out the door) and to both the past and present (experiencing the warmth of friends and family). Grit allows you to continue despite obstacles, to focus on the future, and to accept that it takes effort to achieve meaningful goals. According to the researchers, people who combine these two character strengths have a healthy orientation to the past, present, and future and are therefore resilient and not suicidal.

The *self-determination theory* (Ryan & Deci, 2001) offers a good foundation for the character strengths approach. This theory assumes that people have three innate psychological needs: a need for competence, a need for autonomy, and a need for relatedness. In the character strengths approach, these three requirements are met, thus increasing well-being.

There is no generally accepted classification of character strengths, but some methods are available to identify them: the VIA Signature Strengths test, StrengthsFinder, and the R2 Strengths Profiler (formerly Realise2). These methods are discussed below. Furthermore, the classification of character strengths is likely to change over the years, as does the classification of psychiatric disorders in *The Diagnostic and Statistical Manual of Mental Disorders* (DSM).

The *VIA (Values in Action) Signature Strengths Test* (Peterson, 2006a) aims to develop a universal classification of virtues and character strengths as opposed to the classification of mental disorders in the DSM. There are twenty-four distinct character strengths, divided into six virtues (see Table 1.1). The twenty-four character strengths were deployed in the former *happiness theory* in only the second pillar, engagement (see Chapter 3), in which involvement is the main focus. People can experience flow—time stops for them—if they use their character strengths to meet the challenges in life. In today's well-being theory, the twenty-four character strengths underpin all five pillars. Using them leads not only to engagement but also to positive emotion, meaning, positive relationships, and accomplishment. The VIA questionnaire can be completed online via www.viacharacter.org

TABLE 1.1

Classification of the Six Virtues and Twenty-Four Character Strengths

1. *Wisdom and knowledge* – Cognitive strengths that entail the acquisition and use of knowledge.

- *Creativity* [originality, ingenuity]: Thinking of novel and productive ways to conceptualize and do things; includes artistic achievement but is not limited to it

- *Curiosity* [interest, novelty-seeking, openness to experience]: Taking an interest in ongoing experience for its own sake; finding subjects and topics fascinating; exploring and discovering

- *Judgment* [critical thinking]: Thinking things through and examining them from all sides; not jumping to conclusions; being able to change one's mind in light of evidence; weighing all evidence fairly

- *Love of learning*: Mastering new skills, topics, and bodies of knowledge, whether on one's own or formally; obviously related to the strength of curiosity but goes beyond it to describe the tendency to add systematically to what one knows

- *Perspective* [wisdom]: Being able to provide wise counsel to others; having ways of looking at the world that make sense to oneself and to other people

2. *Courage* – Emotional strengths that involve the exercise of will to accomplish goals in the face of opposition, external or internal.

- *Bravery* [valor]: Not shrinking from threat, challenge, difficulty, or pain; speaking up for what is right even if there is opposition; acting on convictions even if unpopular; includes physical bravery but is not limited to it

- *Perseverance* [persistence, industriousness]: Finishing what one starts; persisting in a course of action in spite of obstacles; "getting it out the door"; taking pleasure in completing tasks

- *Honesty* [authenticity, integrity]: Speaking the truth but more broadly presenting oneself in a genuine way and acting in a sincere way; being without pretense; taking responsibility for one's feelings and actions

- *Zest* [vitality, enthusiasm, vigor, energy]: Approaching life with excitement and energy; not doing things halfway or halfheartedly; living life as an adventure; feeling alive and activated

3. *Humanity* – Interpersonal strengths that involve tending and befriending others

- *Love*: Valuing close relations with others, in particular those in which sharing and caring are reciprocated; being close to people

- *Kindness* [generosity, nurturance, care, compassion, altruistic love, "niceness"]: Doing favors and good deeds for others; helping them; taking care of them

- *Social intelligence* [emotional intelligence, personal intelligence]: Being aware of the motives and feelings of other people and oneself; knowing what to do to fit into different social situations; knowing what makes other people tick

4. *Justice* – Civic strengths that underlie healthy community life

- *Teamwork* [citizenship, social responsibility, loyalty]: Working well as a member of a group or team; being loyal to the group; doing one's share

- *Fairness*: Treating all people the same according to notions of fairness and justice; not letting personal feelings bias decisions about others; giving everyone a fair chance

- *Leadership*: Encouraging a group of which one is a member to get things done and at the same time maintaining good relations within the group; organizing group activities and seeing that they happen

5. *Temperance* – Strengths that protect against excess

- *Forgiveness*: Forgiving those who have done wrong; accepting the shortcomings of others; giving people a second chance; not being vengeful

- *Humility*: Letting one's accomplishments speak for themselves; not regarding oneself as more special than one is

- *Prudence*: Being careful about one's choices; not taking undue risks; not saying or doing things that might later be regretted

- *Self-regulation* [self-control]: Regulating what one feels and does; being disciplined; controlling one's appetites and emotions

6. *Transcendence* – Strengths that forge connections to the larger universe and provide meaning

- *Appreciation of beauty and excellence* [awe, wonder, elevation]: Noticing and appreciating beauty, excellence, and/or skilled performance in various domains of life, from nature to art to mathematics to science to everyday experience

- *Gratitude*: Being aware of and thankful for the good things that happen; taking time to express thanks

- *Hope* [optimism, future-mindedness, future orientation]: Expecting the best in the future and working to achieve it; believing that a good future is something that can be brought about

- *Humor* [playfulness]: Liking to laugh and tease; bringing smiles to other people; seeing the light side; making (not necessarily telling) jokes

- *Spirituality* [faith, purpose]: Having coherent beliefs about the higher purpose and meaning of the universe; knowing where one fits within the larger scheme; having beliefs about the meaning of life that shape conduct and provide comfort

StrengthsFinder (designed in the 1990s by Clifton for Gallup) distinguishes between *talents and strengths*. A talent is a natural recurring pattern of behavior that can be used productively. A strength is the ability to excel consistently on a task. Talents can develop into strengths by learning and practicing. StrengthsFinder 2.0 differentiates between thirty-four talents and can be completed online at www.strengthsfinder.com.

The *R2 Strengths Profiler* (formerly *Realise2*) (hosted by the Centre for Applied Positive Psychology) was developed by Linley et al. (2010) as a strengths assessment and developmental tool. Linley (2008) defined strength as a pre-existing capacity for a particular way of behaving, thinking or feeling that is authentic and energizing to the user, and enables optimal functioning, development and performance.

Linley et al. (2010) distinguished as many as sixty strengths, such as action, adventure, and authenticity. The sixty strengths are assessed according to the three dimensions of energy, performance, and use. To call something a strength, two conditions must be met: competence and energy. Thus, a strength is something you're good at and gives you energy. Linley and colleagues distinguished *potential strengths* (unrealized strengths) from *manifest strengths* (realized strengths). R2 gives a unique and comprehensive perspective on people's capabilities and growth potential. The test is available online at www.capp.co/R2StrengthsProfiler.

APPLICATION 1. LOOK FOR CHARACTER STRENGTHS

Everyone possesses character strengths. Consider what character strengths your clients have. Invite them to build their *top five* signature strengths (or complete the VIA survey) and find out how they can apply these strengths as much as possible in their work and personal life. When they use their character strengths as much as possible, they will definitely increase their well-being.

APPLICATION 2. REGISTER CHARACTER STRENGTHS

Invite clients to create a system to keep track of their experiences each day. Ask them to take one or two character strengths and use them per hour or per half day. Perhaps they can use an alarm clock or another external memory device to identify the character strengths they use per hour. If the strength is playfulness, for example, clients may monitor how often they apply their strength per half day.

APPLICATION 3. TALK ABOUT STRENGTHS

Invite clients to talk about their character strengths and tell stories about how their strengths have been helpful and played a part when they were at their best. Ask them to use their strengths in conversations. For example, if they want to expand their curiosity, invite them to ask questions with sincere concern.

Research on *capitalization*, telling others about positive events (see Chapter 4), shows that this creates a greater effect than the positive impact of the event itself. To share positive events with others, it is necessary that the event be retold so that the event can be relived. Retelling the event ensures that the experience is a longer one and is better preserved in one's memory. In this way, capitalization enhances personal and social resources (Gable, Reis, Impett, & Asher, 2004).

APPLICATION 4. CREATE A STRENGTH ROADMAP

Invite clients to develop strengths through investing time and energy in personal and professional development. The five steps are having them:

1. Identify their character strengths (e.g., by filling out the VIA survey)
2. Get to know their signature strengths (e.g., by discussing the survey with people who know them well to see if they agree with the results)
3. Learn to use their strengths (e.g., by putting their strengths to use and identifying previous successes in using their strengths)
4. Determine their development (e.g., by making a list of all the things they would like to do and than making a selection)
5. Further develop their strengths (e.g., by making concrete plans and taking action)

APPLICATION 5. NOTICE WHAT SHOULD NOT CHANGE

Invite clients to notice everything that is going well in their life and does not need to change or should not change. Which character strengths are they using to accomplish this?

APPLICATION 6. OBSERVE BETTER MOMENTS

Invite clients to observe the better moments in their life, work, sports, or school. What exactly makes one moment better than the other? From a solution-focused perspective, they should do more of what works, and if something is not working, do something else (Bakker, Bannink, & Macdonald, 2010; Bannink, 2007a, 2007b, 2010a).

APPLICATION 7. LIST FIFTY POSITIVE THINGS

Do you remember Paul Simon's song "Fifty Ways to Leave Your Lover"? In this application, clients are invited to list 5 x 10 = 50 positive things to promote their well-being. It's nice to talk about those fifty things with a partner, children, or colleagues and also ask for their fifty positive things:

1. Ten personal character strengths;
2. Ten successes in their life;
3. Ten ways in which they are kind to others;
4. Ten windfalls in their life;
5. Ten ways that others support them.

Areas of Positive Psychology

PP has an increasing number of applications. The areas of psychology and psychiatry, organizations, education, technology, journalism, sports, and society are described, followed by some general applications.

Psychology and Psychiatry

In psychology and psychiatry, until recently the focus was on pathology and disorders and how they could be reduced. According to Seligman, the goal was "to make miserable people less miserable." Success in psychotherapy consisted of the reduction of symptoms—how to pull the client from a negative place—but there was no focus on how the client could reach a positive place (where well-being is found).

Since PP was introduced, professionals have begun focusing increasingly on strengths rather than weaknesses and on positive, functional, and health-promoting factors. Instead of dwelling on what is going wrong, the focus is increasingly on what is going well and which factors promote well-being. Instead of focusing on the causes and consequences of, for example, anxiety or depression, PP focuses (more) on moments when the symptoms are less or do not occur (exceptions to the problem) and what strengths clients use to achieve that. Saleebey (2007) called this the *strength-perspective* with the following assumptions:

- Despite life's struggles, all people possess strengths (i.e. resources) that can be marshalled to improve the quality of their lives. Therapists should respect these strengths and the directions in which clients wish to apply them.

- Client motivation is increased by a consistent emphasis on strengths as the client defines them.
- Discovering strengths requires a process of cooperative exploration between client and therapist; expert therapists do not have the last word on what clients need to improve in their lives.
- Focusing on strengths turns therapists away from the temptation to judge or blame clients for their difficulties and toward discovering how clients have managed to survive, even in the most difficult circumstances.
- All environments—even the most bleak—contain resources.

Examples of psychotherapy in which this *strength-perspective* is used are solution-focused brief therapy (Bannink, 2007a, 2007b, 2010a), positive cognitive behavioral therapy (Bannink, 2012, 2014a), and psychotherapy for posttraumatic success (Bannink, 2008a, 2014b). Bannink and Jackson (2011) compared PP and solution-focused interviewing and concluded that there are differences as well as similarities. However, they can complement and reinforce each other. The aim of both movements is the absence of pathology and the presence of happiness and well-being.

Rashid (2009) mentioned four implications with regard to psychotherapy:

1. Positive interventions do not mean that other interventions are negative.
2. People quickly get used to new conditions. To experience more

well-being, people should engage in activities that fit their values, strengths, and interests.

3. It is intended that PP interventions invite people to engage rather than prescribing what they should do. They should also be undertaken while paying attention to individual and cultural differences related to happiness and well-being.

4. PP interventions are meant not only for people with problems or disorders; PP is also about work, education, understanding, love, growth, and play.

The Workplace

PP is increasingly being used in organizations. Positive features of the workplace and of employees affect their motivation and performance (A. B. Bakker & Derks, 2010). Resources put into effect a positive process in which employees may experience positive emotions, see their work as meaningful, and become enabled to take on challenges. Organizations can provide such resources for their employees, including opportunities for contact and feedback, variety, and autonomy. Employees can also mobilize their own personal resources, such as *job crafting* (Wrzesniewski, LoBuglio, Dutton, & Berg, 2013). Job crafting captures the active changes employees make to their own job designs in ways that can bring about numerous positive outcomes, including engagement, job satisfaction, resilience, and thriving. This ensures that they remain engaged and inspired and perform optimally.

Two questions are important when it comes to the relationship between positive health and work: how to keep employees healthy, and how the human potential in the workplace can be strengthened. Companies can get a lot in return in terms of both improvement in their bottom line (as a result of reduced absenteeism and increased productivity and creativity) and increased job satisfaction and well-being for employees. Work can be both a place to make money and a source of health, job satisfaction, pleasure, involvement, and meaning. Hodges and Asplund (2010) found that the use of character strengths in the workplace ensures an increase in employee engagement, a reduction of staff turnover, and an increase in productivity.

Meyers, van Woerkom, and Bakker (2013) conducted a literature review and found that PP applications in the workplace accounted for more well-being and better performance of the employees. They also provide less stress and burnout and even, to some extent, reduce depression and anxiety in employees.

The army is a special working environment. Seligman (2011) developed a specific training for U.S. forces to promote resilience (*soldier mental fitness*) with the theme "Strong body, strong mind." The first effects were positive; after the training, deployed soldiers experienced less anxiety and depression.

Appreciative Inquiry (AI) is a method to achieve change in organizations (Cooperrider & Whitney, 2005). AI assumes that optimal functioning of individuals and organizations can only be achieved by increasing their strengths, never by repairing their weaknesses. AI is based on bringing out the best in people, organizations, and their surroundings. It is about discovering how an organization looks when it is most alive, most effective, and works at its best economically, environmentally, and socially. Instead of denial, criticism, and searching for causes of problems, it focuses on discovering, dreaming, and designing. AI assumes that every living system is able to tell many rich and inspiring positive stories.

In contrast to the traditional "problem solving," AI does not focus on problems but on the positive elements present within each organization. In addition, an essential difference is that AI involves all employees from the start of a change process. This allows for realizing large changes in a very short time, since support is at its maximum.

When an organization has to deal with dissatisfied customers, for example, AI does not ask, "What are we doing wrong that makes our customers dissatisfied?" but rather "When have our customers been really pleased with our company?" A team is not asked, "How come you are arguing so much?" but rather "Tell me about your team when it's at its best." The focus is on creating a positive working environment in which there is no punishment for what is wrong but appreciation of what is right.

AI uses four stages, called the *4D cycle*: Discover, Dream, Design, and Destiny. Discover is about discovering what is best in an organization. Dream is about how the organization functions when it is at its best and flourishing. This dream is converted into a concrete plan of action (Design) that should lead the organization to the their dreamed goal (Destiny).

Instead of focusing 80 percent on problems, what is not working, and error reduction and 20 percent on successes and what works, AI reversed this *deficit rule* (Cooperrider & Godwin, 2011; see Chapter 6). The *80-20 deficit rule* is still prevalent in the media, health services, and society in efforts to bring about change. By turning around this rule, problems or crises are not ignored (the focus is still 20 percent on challenges), but the main focus (80 percent) is on signs of progress, successes, strengths, and solutions. Drucker (2002), an influential management consultant, suggested that the great task of leadership is to create an alignment of strengths so that weaknesses become irrelevant.

Stam and Bannink (2008) described the vision of a *solution-focused organization*, in which overlap with PP can be found. How can an organization and its employees make the greatest difference to their clients and/or customers? Stam and Bannink discussed basic rules of solution-focused thinking and its role in a solution-focused organization.

The research institute Gallup looked at leadership. They asked 10,000 employees why they actually follow a leader. It was found that executives are more effective if they (continue to) invest in the strengths of their employees; employee engagement is then eight times higher. These executives build teams in which knowledge and skills complement each other and are in balance. Moreover, they understand the needs of their employees, the most important being trust, compassion, stability, and hope (Rath & Conchie, 2008).

Bannink (2010c) described how *solution-focused leadership*, where executives focus on everything that works and enable their employees to flourish, invites staff to collaborate optimally. Solution-focused leadership meets the demands of leadership that are expected in the twenty-first century; executives should no longer act as old-fashioned "bosses" but should be flexible enough to manage the challenges and sometimes paradoxical demands confronting them. They need to be both the "leader" who sets goals and measures results and the "servant" who facilitates and invites employees to excel. And they must be able to take any position between these two extremes.

APPLICATION 8. ALLOW PLANTS IN THE WORKPLACE

Knight (Exeter University, UK) found that employees with green plants in the workplace are 15 percent more productive than employees who work in an environment without green plants. Everyone should be able to see the plants from their position. It's simple: Green plants make people happier, and happier people are more productive.

Education

In education, the focus is increasingly on students' strengths and talents and less on their shortcomings. This seems to make students more motivated to achieve their goals than a problem-oriented approach does. The deployment of strengths plays an important role in promoting a positive development curve in young people (Park & Peterson, 2009). Strengths are important for healthy development and personal growth, but also in the prevention of problems such as depression, substance abuse, and bullying (Bolier, Walburg, & Boerefijn, 2013).

There are also developments toward a *positive school*, where the school as a whole contributes to the well-being of pupils and teachers. A positive school approach is a holistic approach that affects both the school climate and school culture so that there is a positive learning environment in which the school community itself can flourish.

Specific criteria for what defines a positive school climate include:

- Norms, values, and expectations support social, emotional, and physical safety.
- People are engaged and respected.
- Students, families, and educators work together to develop and live a shared school vision.
- Educators model and nurture attitudes that emphasize the benefits gained from learning.
- Each person contributes to the operations of the school and the care of the physical environment.

Research into the positive school approach can be found on the website of the Geelong Grammar School in Australia (www.ggs.vic.edu.au). Research shows that students perform better in schools where there is a positive climate (MacNeil, Prater, & Bush, 2009).

A MARK FOR CURIOSITY

Curiosity is a major character strength, belonging to the virtue of wisdom and knowledge (see Table 1.1). In Nepal, children get a school report like anywhere else in the world. But Nepalese children get something extra: a mark for curiosity. The more curious, the better! This is different in some other countries, where teachers or parents may perceive curiosity as undesired.

Technology

Within technology, there is an examination of what good the combination of PP and technology might bring; this is called *positive technology*, in which technological innovation and PP are integrated. Positive technology is about a scientific approach to the use of technology in such a way that the quality of our personal experience is improved (Riva, Banos, Botella, Wiederhold, & Gaggioli, 2012).

Desmet and Pohlmeijer (2013) of the Delft University of Technology in the Netherlands developed *positive design*. Not only do they design things that are beautiful, functional, and sustainable, but the products should also have a positive impact on individual and social well-being. They strongly believe that it is their responsibility as design researchers to generate knowledge that enables designers to formulate effective strategies in contributing to the happiness of people. This knowledge should help designers not only to deliberately create products that allow for meaningful product–user relationships but ultimately also to design products that contribute to a healthy society and make the world a better place. Some of their projects are: designing for personal and environmental well-being; designing programs that help people save money; designing a tailored telehealth device based on psychological profiles of chronic patients, and creating support for local wind-farms.

Technology can be used to (1) boost positive emotions, (2) stimulate involvement and empowerment, and (3) encourage social engagement and connection. An example of the first category is the use of *virtual reality* to evoke a positive mood. Online positive interventions and serious games (for increasing well-being) are an example of the second category (see Chapter 7), while examples of the last category can be found in social media (e.g., Wikipedia). The rise of mobile technology makes it possible to use apps or text messages to increase the commitment to carry out applications for use in (mental) health. The use of *robots* or *social agents* creates opportunities to enhance the well-being of clients (e.g., robots may help with certain exercises).

Journalism

In journalism, a similar trend has become noticable. In Scandinavia and other countries, *constructive journalism* has been evolving since 2007. It is an emerging domain within journalism that is slowly becoming grounded within academia and is based on reporting positive and solution-focused news instead of negative and conflict-based stories. It aims to avoid a negativity bias and incorporates findings from positive psychology research to produce novel frameworks for journalism. Instead of solely reporting on conflicts and problems, constructive journalism aims to gain a more comprehensieve portrayal of the issues at hand. It aims to expose core causes of problems but also to report on emerging ideas and developments to shift society toward more impartial and sustainable paths.

Constructive journalism aims to express how change is possible and highlights the role each member of society may play to foster it. Additionally, it strives to strengthen the ethics code of journalism by avoiding the distortion of information in order to provide a more real portrayal of the world. Constructive journalism attempts to create an engaging narrative that is factually correct without exaggerating numbers or realities. It focuses on people who want to solve problems and build better futures, thus instilling hope and not just fear. The United Nations would like the world's media to also incorporate constructive journalism, offering solutions and positive alternatives to the current menu of relentless doom and gloom.

Sports

In sports, the focus is on functioning optimally and is oriented toward *flow* (Csikszentmihalyi, 1990). Sport has never been preoccupied much with pathology. In the 1960s, Csikszentmihalyi was already studying people who enjoyed the things they did—people with a passion. There were people who were motivated mainly by the activity itself and were not occupied with the longer-term rewards. He interviewed musicians, chess players, mountaineers, and artists. He noticed that painters kept on going and did not seem to pay any attention to hunger, thirst, or fatigue as long as working on their painting was successful. When the painting was finished, they seemed to lose all interest. Flow is so named because some of the people interviewed by Csikszentmihalyi mentioned by way of metaphor a "current that was carrying them."

> I have called this state the *flow experience* because people simply describe their thoughts and actions when they are in that context as spontaneous and effortless, even though what they are doing is often difficult and risky. But at the time it feels as natural as being carried by the flow of a river, a process which does not require effort or control. (p. 389)

Concepts and experiences corresponding with flow are reflected in various religions and spiritual traditions such as Buddhism and Taoism.

TOP PERFORMERS

How do top performers set goals? Barrell, a performance improvement expert working with baseball players from the San Francisco 49ers and the Atlanta Braves, stated that there are "toward goals" and "away goals." Which one you use has quite an impact on performance. Toward goals have you visualize and create connections around where you are going. You are creating new connections in your brain. What is interesting is that you start to feel good at lower levels with toward goals. There are benefits earlier. Away goals have you visualize what can go wrong, which reactivates the negative emotions involved (Barrell & Ryback, 2008).

Society

In society, the promotion of health, well-being, and optimal functioning is of public importance. This task is carried out by organizations such as primary care facilities, hospitals, youth service organizations, schools, government agencies, and others. Methods to mobilize citizens to improve their health include (1) finding exceptions, (2) appreciative inquiry, and (3) positive health surveys. Finding exceptions (*positive deviance*) is about looking for positive exceptions in a community that often develop unexpectedly. The story "Bright Spots" (see below) is a good example of finding exceptions. Appreciative inquiry (see below) takes the positive aspects and qualities of a community as a starting point for change and examines how to extend this. By participating in a positive health survey, citizens search for a shared perspective and focus on achieving a healthy, safe, and happy community.

BRIGHT SPOTS

This is the story about Sternin, who in the 1990s was working for Save the Children. The Vietnamese government had invited the organization to help fight malnutrition. The conventional wisdom was that malnutrition was the result of a number of huge problems: poverty, ignorance, poor sanitation, and lack of access to clean water. According to Sternin, all these problems were TBU: True But Useless. The millions of kids could not wait for those problems to be solved; he wasn't able to fight these causes. Sternin decided to do something else: He traveled to a rural village and met with the local mothers. He went out to weigh and measure every child in the village. The results were surprising: He found kids who were bigger and healthier than others. Sternin searched for bright spots: people whose behaviors created better results than those of others, using the same resources. The bright-spot mothers fed their kids more meals in a day (using the same amount of food). Healthy kids were also actively fed, while unhealthy kids ate on their own. The bright-spot mothers collected shrimps and crabs from the rice fields (considered adult food) and sweet potato greens (considered a low-class food) and mixed them with the rice, making the meal more nutritious.

Sternin ensured that the solution would be a native one. He invited the mothers to practice the new behaviors, and they spread to other villages. The program was hugely successful: over the next six months, 65% of the kids were better nourished and stayed that way, and the program reached 2.2 million Vietnamese people in 265 villages. What is remarkable is that Sternin was no expert and didn't have the answers when he started. But he did have a deep faith in the power of finding positive exceptions: the bright spots (Heath & Heath, 2010).

APPLICATION 9. PUT MODESTY ASIDE

In many cultures, people are not supposed to talk about their successes. That's why we often see our strengths as normal and nothing to brag about if we see them at all. Sometimes, however, it is useful to put modesty aside and examine what qualities and strengths we have. Invite clients to think of positive things regarding:

- Their appearance: What do they like about themselves?
- Their relationships: When are they good to or pleasant toward others? What makes it fun to live with them?

- Their personality: When are they cheerful, friendly, and honest?
- The way others perceive them: What do others appreciate in them? Which compliments do they get?
- Their performance at work or school: When are they at their best?
- Their daily routines/household: What is going well? What are they good at?

If clients can find few or no strengths, invite them to look through a positive lens at themselves and answer the following questions (Bannink, 2009, 2012, 2014b):

- Where do they get the courage to change if they want to?
- How can they make it easier for themselves to change?
- Where did they get these good ideas? How did they develop them earlier?
- How do they manage to keep going?
- When was their last success, and what did they do to make that happen?
- What strengths do they have?
- When did they become aware that they had those strengths?
- When did others become aware that they had those strengths?
- How could they use these strengths more than they already do?
- How would others notice that they are putting their strengths even more to effect?

- What is easy for them that others may find difficult?
- What was easy for them when they were a child?
- If _____ (e.g., a deceased person) could see how they are doing, what would he or she be proud of?
- What would that person say about them, if that were possible?
- What would that person answer when asked how they achieved that?
- How do changes usually take place in their life?
- What is going well, even if only a little bit?
- What in their life do they want to keep as it is?

APPLICATION 11. IMAGINE A FUTURE WITH STRENGTHS

Invite clients to answer the following questions to ascertain how their strengths can also be used in the future:

- What strengths, skills, and resources do they have?
- How have they used these strengths, skills, and resources so far?
- How can they use these strengths, skills, and resources in the future?

APPLICATION 12. CELEBRATE STRENGTHS

Celebrating successes is described in Chapter 6. Invite clients to celebrate their strengths by:

- Devising a positive self-statement and speaking this self-statement out loud a few times every day (e.g., "I am an open and honest person with good friends").

- Writing down a positive self-statement on a card and carrying it with them. Or ask them to stick it on the mirror or kitchen cupboard at home so they can regularly notice it. Many people say it helps if they regularly take a look at something they are satisfied with.
- Choosing three character strengths each day and reflecting on when they have used these strengths or are going to use them. This will help them to build confidence that these strengths are really theirs and increase positive expectations of their effectiveness.

APPLICATION 13. SEARCH FOR PROFESSIONAL STRENGTHS

People use their personal character strengths as professionals as well. Invite clients to consider what three strengths have brought them to where they are now in their profession. Ask them to discuss this with a colleague, and then invite them to ask the colleague what three strengths he or she would attribute to them. Then ask them to change roles. Which three strengths does the colleague sees in himself or herself, and which ones does the client see in him or her? Invite clients to also consider how they may use their strengths even more in the future.

APPLICATION 14. FIND EXCEPTIONS TO THE PROBLEM

Nothing in the world stays the same; *panta rhei*. This means that there are always exceptions to every problem. Invite clients to think about:

- Moments when the problem is or was less of a problem
- Moments when the problem is or was not a problem

- Moments when the problem was there, but they could cope better
- Moments when there was something of what they would like to have instead of the problem

---

THE CHAMELEON

A chameleon changed his mind constantly. He could not decide whether to get out of bed or what to eat for breakfast. He had to choose where and how to eat, afraid of the day that lay ahead. With every emotion, he changed color. When angry, he became red. If he had a cool idea, he turned to ice blue.

Eventually, he decided to go out. Once outside, he was not sure whether he should go left or right. A giraffe said, "Do the same as me. Take a good look around. Pay no attention to everything around you; that only distracts you." The chameleon tried to do what the giraffe did, but doubt kicked in again. He then heard a hyena say, "You have to do what you want to do." He felt ridiculed, became angry, and took a few steps. Then he started to doubt again.

He met a gorilla that said, "You have to find your own way. The answer is inside." The chameleon felt that the gorilla understood him, but then he began to doubt again.

The next animal was a cheetah that said, "First, you wait. Then go for it with everything that is in you."

An owl finally said, "All animals helped a little bit. But there's one thing you've overlooked. You have something the others don't have!" The chameleon looked surprised. The owl continued: "All animals have the color they are; you are the only animal that can change its color. Know your strengths and be proud of them."

The chameleon had worried so much that he forgot to look at his strengths. He felt excited about the appreciation of the owl and understood how he could appreciate himself. It gave him self-confidence. All the way home, he changed color for fun and forgot to feel doubt about what he had to do. He ate his meal and fell asleep happy. He dreamed about a chameleon that knew what he wanted (Bannink, 2007).

2
Positive Emotion

Downward spiral or upward spiral. As I see it, that's your choice.

—BARBARA FREDRICKSON

This chapter describes the first pillar of Seligman's well-being theory: positive emotion. Being able to focus on positive emotions is the ability to be optimistic and view the past, present, and future in a positive perspective. This positive view in life, where there is room for fun and enjoyment, can help us in relationships and work and inspire us to be more creative and take more chances. It is about experiencing positive emotions: To what extent do we feel happy and content?

Until recently, little attention was given to theories of positive emotions. Fredrickson's broaden-and-build-theory of positive emotions is discussed in this chapter, providing ample evidence of the importance of experiencing positive emotions. Many other applications of positivity are described, such as mindfulness, positive imagery, positive journaling, and self-compassion. However, a good balance between positive and negative emotions is important, because negative emotions are as much a part of the richness of life as positive emotions.

Positive Emotion

The pleasant life is about experiencing positive feelings: To what extent do we feel happy and satisfied? In philosophy, *hedonism* is the doctrine within ethics that states that pleasure is the ultimate good and everyone should pursue all immediate pleasures and avoid all immediate pains for themselves. Hedonism goes back to the Greek philosopher Aristippus of Cyrene (435–356 BC), a pupil of Socrates. He considered bodily pleasures to be better than mental pleasures, presumably because they were more vivid or trustworthy. An important question within hedonism is what generates the greatest pleasure.

There is a difference between *pleasurable* experiences and *enjoyable* experiences. Seligman and Csikszentmihalyi (2000, p. 12) stated:

> Pleasure is the good feeling that comes from satisfying needs such as hunger, sex, and bodily comfort. Enjoyment refers to the good feelings people experience when they do something that stretches them beyond what they were and leads to personal growth and long-term well-being.

It should also be emphasized that pleasure in itself can be empty and may lead to feelings of depression (Seligman, 2002). "Positive emotion alienated from the exercise of character leads to emptiness, inauthenticity, depression and, as we age, to the gnawing realization that we are fidgeting until we die" (p. 8). Therefore, we need also to focus on *engagement* (Chapter 3), *relationships* (Chapter 4), *meaning* (Chapter 5), and *accomplishment* (Chapter 6).

THE ANCIENT GREEKS

The ancient Greeks in the third century BC were already discussing the distinction between striving to not experience emotions and striving to have positive emotions. On the one hand, there were the Stoics; they learned to follow reason, to eradicate passion, and to despise suffering. Imperturbability in pain, suffering, or difficulty was the ultimate good: "how not to be unhappy." Absence of unhappiness is achieved by not experiencing emotions.

Alternatively, the Epicureans argued that civilization and the practice of virtue was the ultimate good: "how to be happy." Happiness is achieved by having positive emotions.

WANTING OR LIKING

The limbic system in the brain is linked to feelings, motivation, and memory. There are two subsystems to distinguish: wanting and liking. Wanting ensures that we desire things and inclines us to do things where reward ensues. Liking indicates whether we will become happy or fortunate in what we do and in what we experience. If everything works out, then these two systems cooperate and learn from each other. However, sometimes we want to do things that do not make us happy at all, like become addicted or engage in bad habits or avoid difficult social situations that we had every intention of confronting.

Therefore, according to Litt (2010), the question "What do I want?" is not useful because we focus our attention only on wanting. Better questions would be "What gives me joy?" or "What makes me happy?" To answer those queries, previous experiences are important: "What made me happy in the past?" When you understand the answer to this question, then wanting and liking are better matched and hence you want and do more of the things that make you happy.

APPLICATION 15. ASK WHAT MAKES THEM HAPPY

Ask clients, "What do you enjoy?" "What makes you happy?" It is important to focus on previous positive experiences to find an answer: "What did you enjoy in the past?" "What made you happy then?" Clients may create a list of activities that used to give them a pleasant and happy feeling and engage in some of them every day.

The Broaden-and-Build Theory of Positive Emotions

Until recently, little attention was paid to theories of (building) positive emotions. This may well reflect the spirit of the age, in which most disciplines have focused on problems and negative emotions such as fear, sadness, anger, shame, and guilt. An electronic search of Psychological Abstracts since 1887 turned up 8,072 articles on anger, 57,800 on anxiety, and 70,856 on depression, while only 851 abstracts mentioned joy, 2,958 mentioned happiness, and 5,701 mentioned life satisfaction. In this sample, negative emotions trounced positive emotions by a 14-to-1 ratio! (Myers, 2000).

Positive emotions are less differentiated than negative emotions, and this imbalance is also reflected in the number of words in most languages that describe emotions.

Due mainly to PP, more attention has been given to positive emotions in recent years. The main theory here is the *broaden-and-build theory of positive emotions* (Fredrickson, 1998, 2000, 2001, 2009). This theory explains the function of positive emotions. In contrast to the narrowing of attention and specific action tendencies associated with negative emotions, positive emotions (interest, contentment, enjoyment, serenity, happiness, joy, pride, relief, affection, love) broaden our attention and behavioral repertoire and, as a consequence, build social, intellectual, and physical resources—resources that can become depleted under chronically stressful conditions. In this way, a pleasant interaction with a stranger grows into a friendship and purposeless play turns into a physical training or sports performance.

People who are feeling positive show patterns of thought that are more flexible, unusual, creative, and inclusive. Their thinking tends to be more efficient and more open to information and options. It is suggested that positive emotions enlarge the cognitive context, an effect recently linked to increases in brain dopamine levels.

Thus, positive and negative emotions are different in their links to action. For example, the negative emotion of anxiety leads to the specific fight-or-flight (or freeze) response for immediate survival. To survive, we immediately focus our attention on a specific behavioral response, such as running or fighting, and therefore we do not expand our thinking to other behavioral alternatives. Positive emotions, on the other hand, do not have any immediate survival value, because they take one's mind off of immediate needs and stressors. However, over time, the skills and resources built by broadened behavior enhance survival. Fredrickson proposed that in contrast to negative emotions that narrow our thought-action repertoires and promote immediate survival-oriented behavior, positive emotions broaden our thought-action repertoires and build enduring personal resources physically, intellectually, psychologically, and socially.

When we are experiencing negative emotions that accompany problems, our attention narrows and we limit our behavior repertoire that does not offer solutions; we feel "stuck." The usual approach of trying to find solutions by delving further into the problem—sometimes with the help of the therapist—perpetuates the situation by creating more negative emotions that continue to narrow our attention and further the sense of being stuck. To use the analogy of a funnel, negative emotions ensure that you will sink into the funnel and create a downward spiral, and positive emotions ensure that you can climb out of the funnel and create an upward spiral.

Fredrickson and Branigan (2005, p. 126) stated, "Thus positive emotions not only make people feel good at the present time but also—through their effects on broadened thinking—increase the likelihood that people will feel good in the future." The same applies to more abstract levels of thought. In experiments with triangles and squares, it was found that it depends on the emotional state of people whether they see only details or the bigger picture: the trees or the forest. If you are experiencing negative emotions, you often see only trees. If you experience positive emotions, you can see the trees *and* the forest.

I CAN CHOOSE

The comedian Groucho Marx (2002) once said, "Each morning when I open my eyes I say to myself: 'I, not events, have the power to make me happy or unhappy today. I can choose which it shall be. Yesterday is dead; tomorrow hasn't arrived yet. I have just one day, today, and I am going to be happy in it.'"

APPLICATION 16. INCREASE CREATIVITY

Test how positive emotions enhance your clients' opportunities and creativity. Invite them to have ready a piece of paper and a pen. Then ask them to examine the back of their hand for one minute and describe everything they see: their skin, its color, the veins, the knuckles of their fingers. Then invite them to take the time to create a list of everything they would like to do. Ask them to remember the feeling they had when they looked at their hand and write down what this feeling wants them to do. If the list is ready, ask them to set it aside.

Then invite clients to think for one minute about a pleasant time in their life—a moment when everything went smoothly and they felt really great. Ask them to let this feeling grow and enjoy it for a while. Then ask them again to take the time to make another list of everything they would like to do. Ask them to recall the feeling they had when they remembered the good time and write down everything this feeling wants them to do. When this list is ready, ask them to compare the two lists and count the ideas on each list. Which list is longer?

Fredrickson (2000) tested her theory by showing films to volunteers that evoked either positive or negative emotions. Subjects who felt positive emotions showed increased creativity and were more able to see the bigger picture. Longitudinal studies show that positive emotions play a role in the development of long-term resources, such as psychological resilience and flourishing. Individuals who express or report higher levels of positive emotions show more constructive and flexible coping, more abstract and long-term thinking, and greater emotional distance following stressful negative events.

Furthermore, Fredrickson found that positive emotions also serve as particularly effective *antidotes* for the lingering effects of negative emotions, which narrow individuals' thought-action repertoires. In other words, positive emotions have an *undoing effect* on negative emotions, since positive emotions are incompatible with negative ones. Positive emotions have a unique ability to reduce the lingering cardiovascular after-effects of negative emotions. Beyond speeding physiological recovery, the undoing effect implies that positive emotions should counteract any aspect of negative emotions that stems from a narrowed thought-action repertoire. For instance, negative emotions can sidetrack people toward narrowed lines of thinking consistent with the specific action tendencies they trigger. When angry, individuals may dwell on getting revenge or getting even; when anxious or afraid, they may dwell on escaping or avoiding harm; when sad or depressed, they may dwell on the repercussions of what has been lost.

There are many positive emotions, of which, based on Fredrickson's research (2009), the ten most important are (1) joy, (2) gratitude, (3) serenity, (4) interest, (5) hope, (6) pride, (7) amusement (humor), (8) inspiration, (9) admiration, and (10) love. These emotions are in order of appearance, and love can occur together with all other listed emotions; therefore, Fredrickson named love last. Love is also the most common of all ten positive emotions. Love and the benefits of sharing positive emotions with others (*capitalization*) is described in Chapter 4. However, a warning is in order: Lyubomirsky (2008) found that too much analysis of positive emotions may cause them to disappear.

Fredrickson (2009) reported an impressive number of studies showing a positive correlation between experiencing positive emotions and a better-functioning immune system; less stress; lower blood pressure; less pain; fewer colds; better sleep; less risk of diseases such as hypertension, diabetes, and stroke; more rapid production of new cells in the body and brain; and a longer life.

THE NUN STUDY

And they lived happily ever after. Handwritten autobiographies from 180 Catholic nuns, composed when participants were a mean age of twenty-two years, were scored for emotional content and related to survival during ages seventy-five to ninety-five. A strong inverse association was found between positive emotional content in these writings and risk of mortality in late life. As the quartile ranking of positive emotion in early life increased, there was a step-wise decrease in risk of mortality, resulting in a 2.5-fold difference between the lowest and highest quartiles. Positive emotional content in early-life autobiographies was strongly associated with longevity six decades later (Danner, Snowdon, & Friesen, 2001).

APPLICATION 17. TURN ON POSITIVITY

Invite clients to do this exercise, or do this exercise yourself. We all have the power to turn positivity on and off for ourselves. Experiment with this and turn positivity on right now. Take a moment to notice your physical surroundings. Whether you are in your living room, bathroom, or on the bus or train, ask yourself, "What is right about my current circumstances? What makes me lucky to be here? What aspect of my current situation might I view as a gift to be treasured? How does it benefit me or others?" Taking time to think in this manner can ignite the inner glow of gratitude. Take a few moments to savor and enjoy the good feeling you have created for yourself.

Now turn positivity off. Positivity-spoiling questions include "What is wrong here? What is bothering me? What should be different and better? Who is to blame?" Try asking yourself these kinds of questions, and follow the chain of thoughts they produce and see how quickly your positivity plummets (Fredrickson, 2009).

APPLICATION 18. CREATE A POSITIVE MOOD BOARD

Invite clients to make a positive *mood board*. A mood board is a visualization of a concept, idea, thought, or feeling, often used by designers.

The subject for a mood board could be the preferred situation in the future. Making a digital mood board can be convenient and fast, but a physically constructed mood board often has more impact because it includes multiple modalities (sight, touch, smell).

APPLICATION 19. THINK POSITIVE SELF-STATEMENTS

Invite clients to think of positive self-statements instead of negative ones, such as the examples shown in Table 2.1. In this way, they may begin to experience more positive emotions using a *growth mindset* (see Chapter 6).

TABLE 2.1
Negative and Positive Self-Statements

Negative self-statements	Positive self-statements
I have never done this before.	I see this as an opportunity to learn something.
That is too complicated for me.	I'm going to do this in a different way.
I don't have the means to do this.	Necessity is the mother of invention.
I don't have enough time for this.	I'm going to reconsider my priorities.
I can't do this.	How can I ensure that I will succeed?
That change is too radical.	I'm just going to do it.
Nobody keeps me informed.	I will start communicating.
I won't get better at this.	I'm going to do it again.

Isen (2005) stated that a growing body of research indicates that positive emotions facilitate a broad range of important social behaviors and thought processes. For example, work from approximately the past decade shows that a positive affect leads to greater creativity, improved negotiation processes and outcomes, and more thorough, open-minded, flexible thinking and problem solving. And this is in addition to earlier work showing that a positive affect promotes generosity and social responsibility in interpersonal interactions.

In a negotiation study, positive affect induced by a small gift (a pad of paper) and a few cartoons significantly increased the tendency of bargainers who were face-to-face to reach agreement and to obtain the optimal outcome possible for both of them in the negotiation. Relative to control groups, people in positive-affect conditions had better negotiation outcomes and enjoyed the task more, and they could understand the other person's perspective. In the control group, where no positive emotion was induced, negotiations were often ended without any result, with hostility and no pleasure. This is in contrast to the experimental group, who reported that they had fun during the negotiations and were more empathetic.

THE POWER OF POSITIVE EMOTIONS

Scientists examined the ways physicians make medical diagnoses by having them think aloud while they solved the case of a patient with liver disease. Astonishingly, the research team found that when they gave physicians a small gift—simply a bag of candy—those physicians were better at integrating case information and less likely to become fixated on their initial ideas, coming to premature closure in their diagnosis (Isen, Rosenzweig, & Young, 1991).

APPLICATION 20. LAUGH (MORE)

Everyone knows laughter is healthy. Berk and Tan (1997) studied the human body's response to mirthful laughter and found that laughter helps optimize many of the functions of various body systems. They were the first to establish that laughter helps optimize the hormones in the endocrine system, including decreasing the levels of cortisol and epinephrine, which lead to stress reduction. Their studies show that repetitious "mirthful laughter" causes the body to respond in a way similar to that induced by moderate physical exercise.

They found that laughter also has other advantages: It improves relationships, improves memory, creates resilience, ensures better learning, makes people more attractive, and helps to make the world a better place. As they say, "a day without laughter is a day wasted." So invite clients to seek the opportunities in their life to laugh (even) more.

APPLICATION 21. GET A PET

Pets such as a dog or a cat make people feel less stressed and happier. Invite clients to go for a walk with the dog (and meet other dog owners) or go sit on the couch with the cat on their lap, relaxing and savoring the moment.

APPLICATION 22. LOOK AT GREEN

Invite clients to look (more often) at the color green. Green appears to be the color that makes people most creative. Research shows that patients who had a view from their bed on the green outdoors resided fewer days in the hospital than patients who did not.

One of the main features of the color green (any green, not only the green of nature) is that it automatically attracts attention without requiring any effort. This phenomenon is called *soft fascination*. During the experience of soft fascination, worry and pain temporarily disappear in the background and attention is drawn to something else. Green distracts from illness and death and stimulates reflection. This allows people to "recharge their batteries" and recover from mental fatigue (Berg & Winsum-Westra, 2006).

Mindfulness

Being conscious in the here-and-now, with attention, openness, and without judgment, is called *mindfulness* (Kabat-Zinn, 1994). Meditation techniques are an important part of mindfulness. Through training, the ability to give specific attention to the here-and-now is developed. Research shows that mindfulness contributes to more positive emotions and well-being.

APPLICATION 23. BE MINDFUL

In mindfulness, it is essential to reflect on the here-and-now and how this is continuously changing, whether pleasant, unpleasant, or neutral. With mindfulness, people use their strengths of self-regulation (of attention) and curiosity (being open in the moment). Mindfulness can be done by regular sitting, walking, or eating, or more informally by focusing attention on what people do and experience (e.g., noticing the softness of the sheets in making the bed or listening to the sound of the kibble dropping into the cat's food bowl). Meditation techniques include giving attention to all parts of the body or paying special attention when doing small everyday activities, such as brushing teeth or tying shoelaces.

Clients can communicate in a mindful way. If they talk or listen to someone, they can concentrate on their voice. If they find that their thoughts are wandering, they can bring their attention back to the voice without condemning themselves. And clients can also walk in a mindful way. If they walk outside, ask them to feel how their feet hit the ground and how they put one foot before the other. Invite them to look around them, hear the sounds around them, and savor the moment.

APPLICATION 24. DESIGN A BEAUTIFUL DAY

Invite clients to set aside next Saturday (or another day) and design themselves a beautiful day. Ask them to plan the enjoyable things they will be doing that day, where they will be, and whom they will be with. Ask them to design the beautiful day—or beautiful half day—in a way that uses their personal strengths and talents. If, for example, one of their main strengths is curiosity and love of learning, their day might include a trip to the museum or simply reading a book that they have been meaning to read. When their beautiful day arrives, ask them to employ their savoring and mindfulness skills to enhance these pleasures.

APPLICATION 25. SAVOR PLEASANT MOMENTS

Invite clients to reflect for a couple of minutes on two pleasant experiences or moments of each day and prolong these enjoyable experiences as long as possible. This intensifies positive emotions through focused attention. Reexperiencing and savoring moments may lead to greater happiness and a greater chance that they will savor pleasant moments in the future.

APPLICATION 26. VALUE TIME

Invite clients to imagine that time is a bank account and, each morning, they are credited with 86,400 seconds. If, by the end of that day, they haven't spent some of their credits, those unspent seconds are instantly be deducted from their account. If that were true, what would they do? Probably they would try to use every one of the seconds. So invite clients to enjoy each second of every minute or every hour of every day, because those moments are something that we can never recover.

APPLICATION 27. APPLY LOVING-KINDNESS MEDITATION

Invite clients to find a quiet place where they can sit comfortably without being disturbed. Ask them to rest their hands lightly on their lap, palms up. Ask them to close their eyes and take a few deep breaths and then breath normally. Say to them, "Just let it be, and just continue to observe your breath. The goal in attending to your breath is to practice being present, here and now. There is no need to suppress your thoughts; just let them be and become aware of them as they come and fade away again."

Mindfulness exercises are used to cultivate *loving-kindness*. It is like guided imagery in which clients reflect on positive feelings for others around them. Invite them to first reflect on a person (or animal) for whom they feel warm and compassionate feelings. Once these feelings take hold, creating positivity in them, ask them to gently let go of the image and simply hold the feeling. Then ask them to extend that feeling to themselves, cherishing themselves as deeply and purely as they would cherish their own newborn child. Next, ask them to radiate their warm and compassionate feelings to others, first to someone they know well, then gradually calling to mind other friends and family members and then all people with whom they are connected, even remotely. Ultimately, ask them to extend their feelings of love and kindness to all people and creatures of the earth: May they all be happy (Fredrickson, 2009).

APPLICATION 28. FOCUS ON THE TASTE OF FOOD

Invite clients to focus one minute on the taste of their food. Ask them to try to distinguish the different sensations: Does it taste salty, sweet, bitter, or sour? They may also talk about it while dining with others, using their mindful skills.

APPLICATION 29. USE WU WEI

Changing oneself is often a slow process. Sometimes nothing happens because people want change to be fast. Therefore, it may be helpful to change nothing at all for a while and to endure the situation as it is.

Invite clients to practice doing things slowly. Maybe, as a result, the situation will be more tolerable and they will have more control than they thought they had. Perhaps the situation will improve by itself if they do not do anything for a while. In addition, if they do nothing, they might come up with new ideas that they have overlooked. In Taoism this is called *Wu Wei*: Act without acting, without forcing.

Positive Imagery

Positive imagery is the ability to think back about positive events in the past or to anticipate positive events in the future. In this chapter, the focus is on positive imagery concerning past events. Positive imagery of the preferred future is described in Chapter 3. Positive imagery—sometimes called *positive time* travel—reinforces positive emotions and helps to optimize health and well-being (Veehof, Bohlmeijer & Geschwind, 2013).

APPLICATION 30. LIST THREE BLESSINGS

Invite clients to write down daily three good things that happened each day for a week. This is called the *three blessings exercise.* These three things can be small in importance ("I went to bed early tonight as I had planned") or big ("The guy I've liked for months asked me out"). Next to each positive event, ask them to write about one of the following: How is it that this good thing happened? What does this mean to me? How can I have more of this good thing in the future? Seligman et al. (2005) found that doing this application for just one week ensures that people still feel better six months later, even when they are feeling depressed.

APPLICATION 31. LIST THREE FUNNY THINGS

A variation of the "List three blessings" applications (see Application 30) is to invite clients to write down every night three funny things that happened that day. Ask them to note how it came to pass that these funny things happened and how they might have influenced this. If people can laugh about themselves and their situation, this means they do not take life too seriously. We all know that laughter is healthy and contagious.

APPLICATION 32. USE A REMINDER

Invite clients to use their phone, computer, tablet, or smart watch to remind themselves every day of what and whom they enjoy most in life. Reminding themselves of what is beautiful in life will give them a break from their daily worries.

APPLICATION 33. COLLECT CHAMPAGNE CORKS

Invite clients to follow my lead. If they have been drinking champagne at the celebration of a joyous occasion, ask them to save the cork and write the event on it. Ask them to put the corks in a pretty glass jar and look at them from time to time to reminisce about those beautiful moments.

APPLICATION 34. REMEMBER BEING AT YOUR BEST

Invite clients to remind themselves of a time when they were *at their best*. Ask them to remember where they were, who was there with them, and what they were thinking, doing, and feeling. This could be an experience that brings forth pleasant memories, such as a birthday, a wedding, a job interview, or a time when they accomplished something important in their life. Clients might find benefit in doing this exercise with physical memorabilia—photo albums, trinkets collected from a vacation, trophies or awards, meaningful letters or printed e-mails, or college degrees. After having them recall the event, ask them to take a few minutes to simply bask in the past success and pleasant feelings this experience brings forth in them. Bring their attention to the details and their positive emotions. Don't ask them to analyze the experience so that they are picking the memory apart and trying to figure out why certain things happened; this is often counter-productive with positive experiences and is not truly savoring. Instead, ask them to focus on the "replaying" of the experience. This exercise has been shown to build positive emotions and confidence.

APPLICATION 35. DEFINE SPECIAL MOMENTS

This application builds on research done on the previous exercise (Application 34). The purpose of this exercise is to invite clients to explore their character strengths, to build a bridge between past critical experiences and future possibilities, and to link positive identity formation with character strengths. There are three steps:

1. Name the defining moment; tell the story (e.g., passing an important exam).
2. List the character strengths involved in the story.
3. Reflect on how this story has shaped who they are (their identity) and how has it impacted them to the present day.

APPLICATION 36. PAY ATTENTION TO WHAT IS GOOD FOR YOU

When thinking about what they've done, many people pay attention only to the things that were not good for them, such as drinking too much, worrying, or arguing. Invite clients to pay attention instead to what they have done that is good for them and list at least three things every day:

1. What did they do so far today that is good for them?
2. What more did they do so far today that is good for them?
3. What else?

If clients cannot answer all three questions yet, ask them, "What will you do the rest of the day that is good for you? What else?"

APPLICATION 37. DRAW OR PAINT MOMENTS OF HAPPINESS

Invite clients to draw or paint some happy moments in their life and enjoy the good feeling they get from it or explain these drawings or paintings to the people around them. Or ask them to draw or paint themselves doing something they are proud of.

Positive Journaling

Monitoring thoughts and behavior by writing them down can provide hope and generate positive emotions, especially when it concerns positive cognitions and successful behavior. For example, clients may keep a *positive diary* in which they keep track every day of the things they are thankful for, proud of, or happy about. Grant (2003) found that people who kept a diary in which they wrote down what they experienced—especially in the case of stressful events—showed more self-reflection on a metacognitive level but had less insight into their problems than people who did not keep a diary. He assumed that these people are stuck in the process of self-reflection and of wanting to understand their own behaviors, cognitions, and emotions and are not focused on achieving their goals.

Burton and King (2004) studied the effects of writing three days for twenty minutes about an intense positive event versus a neutral topic. They divided ninety students randomly across both conditions. It turned out that writing about an intense positive event resulted in a better mood and fewer visits to health centers than did writing about a neutral topic.

APPLICATION 38. WRITE ABOUT AN INTENSELY POSITIVE EXPERIENCE

Invite clients to write for twenty minutes on each of three days about *an intensely positive experience.* Ask them to remember the best experiences in their life—their happiest moments. Ask them to describe the experience in as much detail as possible while also writing about the feelings and thoughts they had. Invite them to relive the experience again and savor it.

APPLICATION 39. KEEP A POSITIVE DIARY

Invite clients to write each day about some positive moments in their lives. These moments do not have to be the best and happiest experiences in their life, as in Application 38. Ask them to also write down why they think those positive moments took place and what those moments say about them. One creative client told her therapist that she took photos to record and remember the better moments in her life.

APPLICATION 40. WRITE DOWN WHAT YOU ARE GRATEFUL FOR

There are many things, big and small, for which people can be grateful. Invite clients to describe each week five things for which they are grateful. Emmons and McCullough (2003) found that participants who had done this several weeks experienced significantly more positive emotions. More elaborate gratitude applications are described in Chapter 5.

APPLICATION 41. WRITE DOWN WHAT YOU ARE PLEASED ABOUT—DESPITE WHAT IS HAPPENING OR HAS HAPPENED

Although in difficult times, it may be hard for people to find out what they are pleased about or can be thankful for, this application is often worthwhile (Bohlmeijer & Bannink, 2013). Invite clients every night to answer the following three questions:

1. What did I do today that I am pleased about, despite what is happening or has happened?
2. What did someone else do that I'm pleased about despite what is happening or has happened? Did I respond to that person in such a way that they would do it again?
3. What else do I see, hear, feel, smell, and taste for which I am grateful?

Experiencing *hope* and *gratitude* are two character strengths, which, according to the classification of PP (see Table 1.1), belong to the virtue *transcendence*. According to Fredrickson, they both are part of the ten most important positive emotions (see above). Hope and gratitude and their applications are described in Chapter 5.

Self-Compassion

It is a misunderstanding to think that PP is only about positive things; it also concerns how we deal with suffering and misfortune, where skills like compassion and resilience play a central role. Recovering and resilient people build a gentle relationship with their emotions and have a healthy way of relating to themselves; they go easy on themselves. While we cannot change the gut-level feelings and reactions that our minds and bodies produce, we can change how we respond to these feelings. Most of us are taught that vulnerable feelings are signs of weakness, to be hidden from others at all costs. However, if properly managed, expressing your vulnerability can be a source of strength and confidence. Being kind to yourself is not only providing comfort in the moment; it is also committing, whenever possible, to reducing future instances of suffering. *Compassion* is sensitivity to the suffering of self and others and a commitment to do something about it (Gilbert, 2010). *Self-compassion* encourages a person's drive while also giving it focus and healthy, wholesome boundaries. The *soothing system*, as Gilbert puts it, gives the context for the striving. Increasing self-compassion has positive consequences, such as increased life satisfaction, wisdom, optimism, curiosity, goal setting, social connectedness, personal responsibility, and emotional resilience.

Neff (2011) developed the Self-Compassion Scale (SCS) (see Chapter 7). A meta-analysis of twenty studies shows that a higher degree of self-compassion is linked with less anxiety, depression, and stress (MacBeth & Gumley, 2012). A higher degree of self-compassion is also associated with higher degrees of optimism, gratitude, wisdom, and well-being; improved coping and resilience; and improved health (Barnard & Curry, 2011). According to Neff (2011), self-compassion revolves around three things:

1. *Self-compassion instead of self-judgment.* People who are kind to themselves are tolerant and loving toward themselves when faced with pain or failure. Self-judging people are tough and intolerant toward themselves.
2. *Common humanity instead of isolation.* Common humanity is a perspective that views our failings and feelings of inadequacy as part of the human condition shared by nearly everyone. By contrast, people who isolate tend to feel alone in their failure.
3. *Emotional regulation instead of overidentification.* People who can regulate their emotions take a balanced view and keep their emotions in perspective. They neither ignore nor ruminate on elements of their lives that they dislike. By contrast, overidentified people tend to obsess and fixate on failure and view it as evidence of personal inadequacy.

APPLICATION 42. PRACTICE SELF-COMPASSION

Applications for compassion often use images that soothe the brain and nourish an inner helper. Think of a safe place, or someone who helps you in difficult times.

There are four basic wishes, expressed both to others and to oneself. In the case of themselves, invite clients to say, "May I feel safe," "May I be as healthy as possible," "May I be happy," and "May I live in peace."

APPLICATION 43. SURROUND THE ANXIOUS SELF IN COMPASSION

An important compassionate way to get in touch with different and problematic parts of oneself is imagination. Suppose clients are very afraid of something. Invite them to sit back, engage in their breathing, and imagine themselves as a compassionate person. When they can feel that expanding and growing inside them, then ask them to imagine that they see their anxious self in front of them. Ask them to look at the facial expression of their anxious self and notice the feelings rushing through them. Ask them to just sit quietly, feel compassion, and send compassionate feelings out to their other self. Ask them to surround that anxious self in compassion and understanding of the torment of anxiety. They do not have to do anything else but experience compassion and acceptance of the anxiety. Ask them to imagine giving as much compassion and understanding as that anxious part needs. Then invite them to imagine what happens to their anxious part when it actually has all the understanding and support it needs (Gilbert, 2010, p. 171).

APPLICATION 44. OBSERVE COMPASSIONATE MOMENTS

Invite clients to observe and write down everyday situations in which they receive or give compassion—their compassionate moments. When was someone compassionate with them, and when did they feel compassion for someone else (human or animal)?

APPLICATION 45. BECOME YOUR OWN BEST FRIEND

Often we are very critical of ourselves and use negative self-statements (Application 19 and Table 2.1). We pay attention to the things we did not do right, or did wrong. By changing negative self-statements into more accepting ones, clients can become their own best friends. Invite them to embrace all aspects of themselves without judgment, especially if they tend to reject or scold themselves.

A BUDDHIST TALE

A long time ago in India, there lived a young woman named Kisa. She met a man whom she fell in love with and who also loved her. They married and had a son. They were very happy, watching their son grow. However, at the age of two, the boy suddenly fell ill and died. Kisa's world collapsed. She was overcome by grief so strong that she denied his death altogether. She wandered around, carrying her dead son and asking people desperately for a medicine that would cure him. Eventually, she found her way to the Buddha and asked him to cure her son. The Buddha said with deep compassion, "Yes, I will help you, but I'll need a fistful of mustard seeds for that." When Kisa told him that she was willing to do anything to get the mustard seeds, the Buddha added, "The seeds must be from a house where no one has lost his or her child, spouse, or parents. All the seeds have to be from a house that hasn't been visited by death."

Kisa went from house to house, but in every house, the reply was, "We do have mustard seeds, but there are fewer of us alive than dead." Everyone had lost a father or a mother, a wife or a husband, a son or a daughter. Kisa visited many houses and heard many different stories of loss. After she had visited all the houses in the village, her eyes were opened and she realized that no one is safe from loss and grief—that she wasn't alone. Her grief turned into compassion for the other grieving people. Then she was able to grieve over the death of her son and bury his body (Furman, 1998).

APPLICATION 46.
DISCOVER SELF-COMPASSION IN THE PAST

Invite clients to find times in their life when they were a little nicer to themselves, even if it was only a little bit. What did they do exactly? How did they succeed in doing that? What were the positive consequences? And what small step can they take to increase the chances of more moments of self-compassion?

APPLICATION 47. FIND A SAFE PLACE

This exercise is a good way to reduce stress and anxiety. Invite clients to choose a place where they have been, or an imaginary place, that evokes a sense of peace, calmness, serenity, and security. This may be their own bed, a fantasy island where no person can come unless invited, or a vault in a bank. Ask them to go to that safe place for a few minutes each day and imagine, in great detail, the good feeling it gives them. Clients can use this application with their eyes closed or open, and they can either tell someone else what their safe place is or keep it to themselves.

APPLICATION 48. INCREASE PHYSICAL ENERGY

Invite clients to get enough physical exercise. Ask them to eat healthily, exercise regularly, and get enough sleep. This seems obvious, yet this application often proves easier said than done.

APPLICATION 49. CHOOSE TO BE HAPPY

Invite clients to stop worrying, complaining, and acting grouchy. Ask them to make themselves happy by consciously choosing to embody that feeling for just a few minutes or more. Invite them to be that way and hold that feeling for as long as they can. It actually works!

Another way for clients to feel better is to hold a pencil or pen between their teeth for two minutes (across from cheek to cheek). This simple action forces their mouth and face to smile, and bizarre as it sounds, this increases their dopamine level and has a real effect on their happiness levels.

APPLICATION 50. PLAN PLEASURABLE ACTIVITIES

Invite clients to make a list of pleasurable activities and make sure that every day, in addition to all the things they have to do, they engage in activities they actually want to do. Examples are taking a walk, visiting friends, going to the forest or beach, reading a book, or making a cup of tea or coffee. If possible, have them do an activity they actually want to do following an activity they have to do to find a good balance.

APPLICATION 51. RELAX

Invite clients to just stop all their worrying, for a moment, and think about an image that evokes tranquility. The more realistic the daydream is in color, sound, feel, smell, and taste, the more relaxed the experience will be. Ask them to visualize a peaceful situation or dream landscape. It could be their favorite vacation spot, a penthouse in New York, or something that they can actually touch, such as the feeling of their favorite sweater or pet.

APPLICATION 52. DESIGN A DAILY RITUAL OF JOY

Invite clients to ask themselves when they wake up, "What am I most looking forward to today?" Invite them to ask themselves at the end of the day, "What did I like most today?" Clients may write these down on a piece of paper, put it in a box or jar, and reread the pieces of paper one year later. The advantage of this is that the writing allows them not only to enjoy their daily ritual longer, but also to relive it later. Doing a (joyful) dance every day is also good for one's physical and mental well-being.

APPLICATION 53. FOCUS ON WHAT WORKS

We have a natural tendency to pay more attention to what is not going well than to what is going well. From a solution perspective, invite clients to turn around that focus and give special attention to what works. Whether it is their private life or work, sports or school, invite them to focus on what works instead of what does not work. And invite them to get (even) better at the things they are doing right.

APPLICATION 54. FOCUS ON USEFUL OR FUN THINGS

Invite clients to think about useful or fun things instead of negative things or things they need to do before they fall asleep. Ask them to imagine the excellent presentation they are going to give tomorrow, or the meeting they have planned with a good friend.

They will probably sleep better, because we dream more often about our last thoughts before we fall asleep. The same applies if these are negative thoughts. So ask clients to think about things for which they are grateful, visualize a successful moment tomorrow, or do something that relaxes them.

APPLICATION 55. APPLY THE LOCI METHOD

An approach to overcome negative thoughts is to replace them with positive ones. Depressed people may be able to benefit from this. Invite clients to use the *loci method*, a memory trick for imprinting and remembering positive things. Clients may do this by linking positive events to specific buildings, such as the tower or supermarket they pass every day on their way to work. In this way, they automatically get positive impulses when seeing these buildings. Eventually this application may lift the gloom that surrounds them.

Listening to favorite music, or music that makes one happy, helps to make gloomy or anxious feelings disappear. Invite clients to find out what music is helpful in such situations. Research shows that music reduces depression, anxiety, and acute and chronic pain.

CRISIS

In moments of crisis, professionals often tend to take control. However, even crisis can be handled in an effective solution-focused way. Most people in crisis stabilize when they are invited to focus on what they want to be different and to use past successes and competencies.

A mentally disabled man with autism, in his early forties, lived in an apartment with twenty-four-hour supervision. His girlfriend suddenly ended their relationship. He was very unhappy and wanted to die. The team was worried and feared that hospitalization was needed.

A solution-focused therapist sat down next to him and acknowledged his grief. She asked how his grief could become less, and what he wanted to feel instead. He indicated that he wanted to be happy again. He was also asked what he would do differently when he became happy again. He told her that he liked listening to music. She asked him what music he liked to play when in a good mood. He showed her by turning on the music and playing it softly. Then the therapist suggested that he play the music a bit louder. One thing led to another; he softly began singing along and the volume was turned louder and louder. He was asked how he could prolong the good feeling. He said that he would need some help from the team and that playing music and singing would probably help. The team was called in and, together with the therapist, he explained his plan. For the first time, a smile appeared on his face. The therapist congratulated him on his beautiful music and singing and the fact that he knew exactly what helped him to feel better. The crisis was over. That weekend, loud music was heard often (Roeden & Bannink, 2007).

APPLICATION 57. LEARN TO PLAY AN INSTRUMENT

When people play music, their entire brain lights up because they are using almost every region of the brain. Collins (2014) found that, specifically, the regions dedicated to audio, visual, and motor functions light up. Those regions are naturally strengthened as people practice and play their instrument more and more, and that leads to many benefits outside music. These benefits include better attention to detail, stronger planning and strategic skills, and better memory. So invite clients to learn to play any instrument they like.

Balance Between Positive and Negative Affect

Although everyone is familiar with positive and negative emotions, there sometimes seems to be a little confusion around this topic. Seligman (2011) stated that when he started out as a therapist almost forty years ago, it was common for his clients to tell him that they just wanted to be happy. Seligman transformed this into the clients' wish to get rid of their depression. Back then, he did not have the tools of building well-being at hand and was blinded by Freud and Schopenhauer (who taught that the best humans can ever achieve is to minimize their misery); the difference had not even occurred to him. He had only the tools for relieving depression. But he found that every individual just wants to be happy, and this legitimate goal combines relieving suffering and building well-being. The cure, to his way of thinking, uses the entire arsenal for minimizing misery—drugs and therapy—and also adds positive psychology into the mix.

Of course, negative affect is not always wrong. J. S. Beck (2011) stated that the aim of *cognitive behavior therapy* (CBT) is not to get rid of all distress; negative emotions are as much a part of the richness of life as positive emotions and serve as important a function as does physical pain, often alerting us to potential problems that may need to be addressed. In addition, therapists should seek to increase clients' positive emotions through discussion of their interests, positive events that occurred during the week, and positive memories. Therapists should often suggest homework assignments aimed at increasing the number of activities in which clients are likely to experience mastery and pleasure.

As an example of how negative emotions can be decreased and positive emotions can be propagated, Kranz, Bollinger, and Nilges (2010) examined the relationship between chronic pain and well-being. In their study, 150 patients in pain produced self-reports, monitoring acceptance of pain, positive and negative emotions, and flexibility. They found that the willingness to accept pain, including the recognition that pain was out of control, especially reduced negative emotions, while involvement in activities (the behavioral component of the acceptance of pain to undertake activities in spite of the pain) promoted positive emotions. They also found that being active mediated between the willingness to accept pain and positive emotions. Flexibility, the willingness to adapt personal goals to the situation, promoted both the acceptance of pain and being active, especially in cases of severe pain. In summary, the well-being of chronic pain patients is closely related to continuing with activities, with the underlying factor being that the pain is accepted.

APPLICATION 58. OBSERVE YOUR MOOD

Invite clients to observe their mood for several weeks during various activities of the day. Then ask them to monitor the moments when their mood is (slightly) better and what they do differently at these times. Often doing more of what works is sufficient to feel better.

THE DOG I FEED MOST

An old native Indian described his inner conflict: "There are two dogs living inside of me. One dog is mean and bad; the other is good. The mean dog fights the good dog all the time." His grandson asked which dog would win. The Indian thought for a moment and then said, "The dog I feed most."

APPLICATION 59. CHALLENGE NEGATIVE THOUGHTS

Challenging negative cognitions may be a useful approach with individual clients or with team members. This application is about contradicting negative thoughts as quickly as possible. Ask clients or team members to write down their typical negative thoughts about themselves or the team that pop up in their mind, such as "I will never accomplish anything worthwhile" or "We don't seem to be able to work together." The idea is to write these thoughts on index cards. After they have written the cards with some of their regular negative thoughts, pick one up at random and read it out loud. Then invite them to rapidly dispute the negative beliefs with every argument they can come up with. Is this thought true? Is it helpful? What would be a more positive thought? This is called *Rapid Fire Facts* (Fredrickson, 2009)—people rapidly fire contradicting positive facts at the negative sentence. When they run out of facts, ask them to pick another card and repeat the rapid fire facts. Coming up with contradictory facts will get easier and easier with each card. With this tool, clients become quick at contradicting their negative thoughts.

What we pay attention to grows in our consciousness and in our lives. Focusing on a positive, concrete, and achievable goal—on hope, exceptions to problems, strengths, and past successes—helps to create an atmosphere in which negative affect decreases and positive affect and satisfaction with life increase. These are the three factors that together determine well-being.

We all want to feel pleasure and avoid pain, and although people generally prefer happiness, they sometimes prefer being angry or anxious as they see these emotions as providing long-term benefits. Tamir, Mitchell, and Gross (2008) found that people typically prefer to feel emotions that are pleasant (e.g., excitement) and avoid those that are unpleasant (e.g., anger). They tested whether people prefer to experience emotions that are potentially useful, even when they are unpleasant to experience. They tested whether individuals are motivated to increase their level of anger when they expect to complete a task where anger might enhance performance. Participants were told that they would play either a violent or a nonviolent computer game. They were then asked to rate the extent to which they would like to engage in different activities before playing the game. They found that when participants expected to play a violent game, they preferred activities that were likely to make them angry (e.g., listening to anger-inducing music, recalling past events in which they were angry). In contrast, participants preferred more pleasant activities when they expected to play a nonviolent game.

To examine whether preferences to increase anger resulted in improved performance, participants were assigned at random to either an angry, neutral, or excited emotion introduction and then played a violent and a nonviolent computer game. As expected, angry participants performed better than others in the violent game by successfully killing more enemies. However, angry participants did not perform better than others in the nonviolent game, which involved serving customers. Such findings demonstrate that what people prefer to feel at any given moment may depend, in part, on what they might get out of it. A factor that ought to be considered, where anger is concerned, is that it can be very arousing and thus can feel good in a certain way.

Interestingly, people sometimes opt for less arousing and less pleasant feelings such as fear. This is particularly true when people are pursuing avoidant rather than approach goals. *Approach goals* seek out a positive outcome, such as "I want to go to bed early tonight because I want to feel fit tomorrow morning." *Avoidance goals* seek to avoid a negative outcome, such as "I don't want to go to bed late tonight because I don't want to be sleepy at work tomorrow morning." Tamir and colleagues found that people prefer fear when they are pursuing avoidance goals. Despite the unpleasantness of fear, people appear to recognize that it will help them better achieve certain types of goals.

CONSIDER A SAILBOAT

Consider a sailboat. Rising from a sailboat is an enormous mast that allows the sail to catch the wind. Below the waterline is the keel, which can weigh tons. You can take the mast going up as positivity and the keel down below as negativity. If you've ever sailed, you know that you can't get anywhere without the keel. If you tried, at best you'd slide aimlessly across the water, or at worst you'd capsize. Although it is the sail hanging on the mast of positivity that catches the wind and gives you fuel, it is the keel of negativity that keeps the boat on course and manageable. And just as the keel matters most when you're going upwind, appropriate negativity matters most in hard times (Fredrickson, 2009).

3

Engagement

It is never too late to be who you might have been.

—GEORGE ELIOT

This chapter is about *engagement*, being able to find activities that take our full engagement. Engagement in the activities in our life is important for learning, growing, and nurturing personal happiness. This life of involvement refers to our commitment to do what we do: To what extent do we experience a sense of personal fulfillment?

The basis of the good life is knowing what we are good at—what our signature strengths are—and then arranging our life in all possible areas in such a way that we use these strengths optimally. This allows us to experience *flow*, a condition in which time stops for us because we are really engaged in a challenging task.

In engagement, setting goals is important, as is the idea of personal growth. Setting goals can be achieved by positive imagery of the preferred future. There is a positive correlation between happiness and optimism. Optimism can be influenced by how you behave and what you focus your attention on.

Engagement

Aristotle (384–322 BC) was concerned with answering the question "What is the best way to live?" In his description of the good life, he spoke in terms of *eudemonia*. According to him, this is not the pleasant life as described in Chapter 2. For Aristotle, living well consisted of personal development and excellence of character. In the good life, happiness is sought by experiencing pleasure during moments of contemplation or while having a good conversation. Therefore, engagement does not necessarily correspond with pleasant feelings.

The question is, how can well-being best be pursued? On the one hand, it is assumed that happiness is qualitatively different from eudemonia (Ryff, 1989). In this view, happiness is not an accurate indicator of a good life. On the other hand, it is assumed that one cannot draw a sharp line between happiness and eudemonia and that it is not useful to distinguish these two forms of well-being as separate concepts (Kashdan, Biswas-Diener, & King, 2008).

Seligman stated in a TED talk (TED.com, 2004) that engagement and meaning (see Chapter 5) are far more important for well-being than positive emotions, which are only "the whipped cream and the cherry on the cake."

Flow

The basis of the good life is, as mentioned before, knowing your signature strengths and shaping your life in such a way that you use these strengths as much as possible. In the good life, you are not aware of yourself while performing a challenging task; you are experiencing *flow*. You may feel at one with music, or experience flow while writing (like me) or engaging in sports; you lose your self-consciousness while doing something you find interesting. In essence, flow is characterized by complete absorption in what you do. It is the perception that time stands still, where you feel completely at ease, negative emotions like embarrassment are absent, and you are engrossed in what you do. This is different from experiencing positive emotions, because there are no positive emotions during flow. Usually you do not experience any emotions. Only afterward do you experience emotions; for example, you may feel satisfied with or proud of what you've done.

According to Nakamura and Csikszentmihalyi (2005) flow is characterized by at least some of the following aspects:

- Intense and focused concentration on the present moment
- Merging of action and awareness
- A loss of reflective self-consciousness
- A sense of personal control or agency over the situation or activity
- A distortion of temporal experience (i.e., one's subjective experience of time is altered)

■ Experience of the activity as intrinsically rewarding, also referred to as *autotelic experience*

APPLICATION 60. EXPERIENCE FLOW

When you are experiencing flow, you feel challenged and make use of your full capabilities. You can experience flow in almost anything, but depending on your history and circumstances, almost anyone can also experience boredom or anxiety. It is the subjective challenge and subjective skills that determine the quality of the experience. In addition, attention plays an important role, both in getting into flow and maintaining flow. Some activities are structured in such a way as to enhance the possibility of flow, such as sports and games, where the mentioned characteristics are often naturally present.

Flow can also be achieved by getting control over your thinking, as in meditation or prayer. Invite clients to consider what activities they like and are good at and see as a challenge, because that is when the chances of experiencing flow are the highest (Bannink, 2009, 2016).

APPLICATION 61. ANSWER THREE QUESTIONS TO BUILD HAPPINESS

Invite clients to ask themselves these three questions each day to build happiness:

1. What did I do today that I feel good about?
2. What has someone else done that I am happy with? Did I react in

such a way that this person will perhaps do something like that again?

3. What else do I see, hear, feel, smell, or taste that I like?

Setting Goals

An important dimension of the good life is setting goals: having plans for the future and the idea that your life has direction (Ryff, 1989). Another dimension of well-being is the idea of *personal growth*: You see development in your life, and you see yourself as growing and open to new experiences and opportunities.

There is a positive relationship between setting goals and well-being. Identifying and pursuing goals ensures commitment and fosters the idea that what you're doing makes sense. By working on goals, you also have the idea that you can exercise some degree of influence on the environment, creating a positive self-image and positive emotions (Brandtstädter & Rothermund, 2002). You also experience progress—approaching the goal—as rewarding and positive in itself. It is important that these are goals you can identify with or enjoy (Bode & Arends, 2013). It is advisable to not seek short-term or hedonic goals as such, but to aim for long-term goals and (social) goals that transcend you.

ARISTOTLE

The Greek philosopher Aristotle (1998) used to say that having a goal is important. "A happy person is like a stone that falls to the ground and stays there quietly. After all, everything and everyone on earth pursues a goal, which is somewhere hidden inside of him. A stone wants to fall on the earth. Fire wants to go up into the sky. A person wants to be happy. If that person has developed his inner talents—his intellectual characteristics and traits—in the right way, then he has achieved the good life and is happy."

People may create three types of narratives (life stories) about their own and other people's lives:

1. A progressive narrative, from which one concludes that people and situations get closer to their goal
2. A stable narrative, from which one concludes that there is no movement
3. A digressive narrative, from which one concludes that people and situations are getting away from their goal

APPLICATION 62. CHANGE A NEGATIVE INTO A POSITIVE NARRATIVE

This application shows how one can change a stable or digressive narrative into a progressive one. Usually people think of blame and guilt in a negative sense. Perhaps this is because they have never heard of *positive blame*. When thinking of exceptions to the problem, of past successes, of strengths or skills, people are using a form of positive blame: placing the responsibility for positive results on the person who achieved the good things.

Invite clients to answer, "How did you do this?" "How did you come up with that good idea?" The message is that everyone has certain skills and that people can—if applicable—repeat their successes.

APPLICATION 63. FORMULATE A GOAL

Invite clients to formulate a goal. First ask them to choose any subject/field or skill they want to become really good at. Then ask them to make a list of all the things they would like to do and experience in their life—everything they want to achieve. Then ask them to reduce that list to only those goals that motivate them the most. Finally, ask them to think of activities that would start moving them toward their goal.

THE CHESHIRE CAT

The following conversation shows that when the goal is not clear, clients might not reach it and might possibly end up somewhere else. The Cheshire Cat is a fictional cat popularized by Carroll's depiction of it in *Alice's Adventures in Wonderland* (1865, p. 43) and known for its distinctive mischievous grin. Alice encounters the Cheshire Cat outside on the branches of a tree, where it appears and disappears at will.

Alice: Would you tell me, please, which way I ought to go from here?

The Cat: That depends a good deal on where you want to get to.

Alice: I don't much care where.

The Cat: Then it doesn't much matter which way you go.

APPLICATION 64. SCALE PROGRESS

In terms of progress, most people are not at a complete zero when they set a goal. Therefore, invite clients to explore on a scale of 10 to 0, where 10 means that the goal is fully achieved and 0 the opposite, how far they have come. If, for example, they rate their current situation at a 3, ask them to figure out how they got there and what enables the situation to be at a 3 and not lower. Read the story below about the car wash and how people find it more motivating to be partly finished with a longer journey than to be at the starting gate of a shorter one.

AT THE CAR WASH

A car wash ran a promotion featuring loyalty cards. Every time customers bought a car wash, their card was stamped, and when they had eight stamps, they got a free wash. Other customers got a different loyalty card. They needed to collect ten stamps (rather than eight) to get a free car wash—but they were given a "head start": Two stamps had already been added.

The goal was the same: Buy eight additional car washes, get a reward. But the psychology was different: In one case, you're 20 percent of the way toward the goal; in the other case, you're starting from scratch. A few months later, 19 percent of the eight-stamp customers had earned a free wash versus 34 percent of the head-start group (and the head-start group earned the free wash faster).

Goldstein, Martin, and Cialdini (2007) found that people find it more motivating to be partly finished with a longer journey than to be at the starting gate of a shorter one. To motivate action is to make people feel as though they're closer to the finish line than they might have thought. "When soliciting another person for help with anything, you should try to point out how that person has already taken steps towards the completion of that task" (p. 159).

APPLICATION 65. CREATE A CARTOON

Ask a child you work with if he or she loves animals; usually this is the case. Together create a cartoon with six pictures, in which the child first draws the last picture—number 6—as the animal he wants to be in the future, such as a lion or elephant. Usually children come up with big, strong animals. Then ask the child to draw the first picture—number 1—as the animal he is now, maybe a mouse or a turtle. This is usually a small, sometimes frightened animal. Afterward, have the child draw the intermediate pictures, in which the animal changes in the direction of the goal (the animal the child wants to be in the future). In this activity, together with the child (and the parents), the professional "translates" the pictures into the real world of the child. Remember to ask which qualities and character strengths of the first animal the child will take with him or her when changing into the desired animal.

This application can also be done with a team or group. In this instance, generally speaking, no animal pictures are used; the six pictures in the cartoon are drawn about whatever the team or group comes up with.

Positive Imagery

Imagery interventions can be used to remove and transform negative images or create and build positive ones. *Positive imagery* is used in goal setting, in skills training, and in checking, appraising, and adjusting to solve problems and fine-tune skills. All three elements are central to creating "new ways of being," a new orientation that clients, who have previously held strong persistent negative beliefs, are encouraged to develop toward themselves. The focus is on envisioning new ways of being or desired states. For example, treating oneself with kindness and compassion rather than disgust may create fundamental changes. Since imagery has a more powerful effect on positive emotion than verbal thoughts about the same information, strategies in which imagery is used appear to be particularly useful tools for generating positive new ways of being (Hackmann, Bennett-Levy, & Holmes, 2011). Einstein (1954) knew this and wrote, "Imagination is more important than knowledge because knowledge is limited." In Chapter 2, it was stated that positive imagery can enhance positive emotions and help to optimize health and well-being. In that chapter, positive imagery was used to look back at what was. This chapter discusses positive imagery to envision the preferred future—no looking back, just looking ahead. Imagining a positive future corresponds with more optimism (Meevissen, Peters, & Alberts, 2011), growth of mental health (Allemand, Hill, Ghaemmaghami, & Martin, 2012; Emmons, 2009; Hoppmann & Blanchard-Fields, 2010), and enhanced meaning (Hicks, Trent, Davis, & King, 2012). Positive imagery of the preferred future also helps in eliciting positive emotions during stressful events (MacIntyre & Gregersen, 2012) and has a positive impact on motivation and learning (Simons, Vansteenkiste, Lens, & Lacante, 2004). Emmons (2003, p. 3) stated that there is a link between having goals and a subsequent orientation toward the future: "There is perhaps no characteristic more fundamentally human than the capacity to imagine future outcomes and to devise means to attain these outcomes."

APPLICATION 66. USE MENTAL CONTRASTING

Oettingen (1999) and Oettingen, Hönig, and Gollwitzer (2000) described the technique of *mental contrasting* as applied to goal setting. Mental contrasting is an expectancy-based route and rests on mentally contrasting fantasies about a desired future with negative aspects of the present reality which are seen as obstacles, and emphasizes the necessity to change the negative present reality to achieve the preferred future. This necessity to act stimulates relevant expectations of success, which then informs goal commitment. The authors stated that reversing this order (i.e., reverse mental contrasting) by first elaborating the negative reality followed by elaboration of the preferred future—as is usually done in traditional psychotherapies—fails to elicit goal commitment congruent with expectations of success.

Invite clients to grab a pen and paper or computer and do the following:

- Write down the goal they want to achieve (e.g., being more productive at work).
- Describe the positive consequences of achieving that goal (e.g., feeling satisfied at the end of the day).
- Relax for a moment and visualize as vividly as possible how it will be when they succeed and they feel satisfied.
- Describe an obstacle in their path towards the goal (e.g., spending too much time on Facebook).
- Write down when and where this obstacle is most likely to occur (e.g., when feeling tired).
- Write down how they can overcome the obstacle (e.g., by standing up and stretching a bit).
- Write down their plan in an *if-then format*. Make sure they name a specific time and place (the "if" part) and a specific behavior (the "then" part). For example: "*If* I get tired of working on my computer (an obstacle, where and when), *then* I will get up and stretch for a while (a specific behavior to overcome the obstacle)."

APPLICATION 67. VISUALIZE A BEST POSSIBLE SELF

Invite clients to take a moment to imagine a future in which they are bringing their *best possible self* forward. Ask them to visualize a best possible self that is very pleasing to them and whom they are interested in. Also ask them to imagine that they have worked hard and succeeded at accomplishing their life goals. You might think of this as the realization of their life dreams and of their own best potential. The point is not to think of unrealistic fantasies but rather things that are positive, attainable, and within reason. After they get a fairly clear image, invite them to write about the details.

Invite clients to then visualize this future for two weeks every evening (e.g., before going to sleep). Ask them to each night focus on different domains within the scene, such as their personal life, relationships, work, or study, to prevent the reduction of the effectiveness of the visioning. Writing their thoughts and hopes down will help them to create a logical structure and help them move from the realm of foggy ideas and fragmented thoughts to concrete, real possibilities. Research shows that repeated visualization enhanced optimism, and this optimism continued even after the intervention period was over (Meevissen et al., 2011).

YOUR BEST POSSIBLE SELF

King (2001) asked eighty-one participants to write on four consecutive days for twenty minutes. The participants were randomly assigned to four conditions: writing about the most traumatic event in their lives, writing about their "best possible self" (see Application 67), writing about a combination of the two, or writing about a nonemotional subject (the control group wrote about their plans for that day). Their mood was monitored before and after the writing, and information was collected on the health of all participants. After three weeks, their subjective well-being was measured. Participants who wrote about their goal in life (their "best possible self") were significantly less distressed than those who wrote about the trauma, and they also reported a significant increase in well-being. After five months, a significant interaction was found: Participants who wrote about either the trauma or their "best possible self," or both, were ill less often than the control group.

APPLICATION 68. ASK THE MIRACLE QUESTION

Another way to describe the preferred future is to ask clients the *miracle question* (Shazer, 1985; Jong & Berg, 2002). Invite clients to imagine that a miracle happens tonight while they are sleep and the problem that brings them here today has been solved (to a sufficient degree), but they are unaware of it because they were asleep. What will be the first thing they will notice tomorrow morning that will tell them that this miracle has happened? What will they do differently? What else? How will the rest of the day look like? How will other people (family, colleagues, friends) find out that the miracle has happened? How will they react (differently)?

A variation of the miracle question is, "Suppose tonight a miracle happens (and the rest of the miracle question) and tomorrow you are 'at your best.' What will you or important others notice during the day about you being at your best?"

APPLICATION 69. WRITE A LETTER FROM THE FUTURE

Invite clients to write a *letter from their future* to their current selves. Ask them to say that they are doing fine and describe where they are, what they are doing, what they have gone through to get there, and so on. Ask them to tell themselves the crucial things they realized or did to get there. Finally, ask them to give their present selves some sage and compassionate advice from the future (Dolan, 1991, 1998).

APPLICATION 70. START AT CHAPTER TWO

Invite clients to do this application by saying to them, "A book is made up of many chapters. You can see your own life in this way. If you were to write the story of your life, you could start with the second chapter instead of starting at chapter one. Any problems that you are currently experiencing can be omitted. What positive differences will there be in your life description? How different will you feel? Which people will you omit, and which will you include to make them part of chapter two? Which strengths and resources do you have in chapter two? Which good ideas from chapter two could you already start using? Please write your own life story, but start at chapter two."

Invite clients to imagine that many years later they are an *older and wiser version of themselves*. They are still healthy and have all intellectual capabilities. They may ask this older and wiser version of themselves questions like:

- If they look back on their life, what advice would they give to their younger version?
- If they look back on their life, what do they like most about the life they have lived?
- Is there anything they would rather have done differently?
- What do they hope their children would like to remember about their life with them?
- On a scale from 10 to 0, to what extent have they achieved these wishes in their present life?
- What would be the smallest step they can take to reach a higher mark (if they want to reach this)?
- How, from this older and wiser person's view, could therapy (if needed) be most useful to them?

Clients can also go for a walk with the older and wiser version of themselves while asking for advice regarding a problem. What do they think this old and wise person would advise them to do in order to get through the present (difficult) phase of their life? What would this person say that they should be thinking of? What would this person say that would help them the most to recover from the past? What would this person say about how they can console themselves?

APPLICATION 72. SPEND TIME WITH AN OLDER VERSION OF YOURSELF

An alternative to *imagining an older and wiser version of yourself* is an application I heard about during a workshop by Lopez at the IPPA 2013 conference: *entering the aging booth*. It comes down to this: Invite clients to imagine they are ten or twenty years older and living a life that they would like to lead. "Spending time with an older version of yourself" is a nice way to imagine the preferred future, but it does not connect this future to a current (problematic) situation as the application "Imagine an older and wiser version of yourself" (number 71) does.

APPLICATION 73. THANKS FROM YOUR FUTURE SELF

Invite clients to do something each day for which their future self will thank them. Ask them to take good care of themselves and find things they can do today, such as taking a walk, eating healthy food, learning something new, or doing something nice for someone else.

APPLICATION 74. PLAN A VACATION

Invite clients to plan a holiday, because this creates an increase in positive emotions. A holiday mindset begins long before it actually takes place and provides a positive "halo effect." Regularly taking a holiday may reduce stress and depression, enhance positive emotions, and improve health. Especially when it's cold, wet, and dark outside, planning a holiday has favorable effects.

APPLICATION 75. DESCRIBE A YEAR LATER

Invite clients to describe a day a year later than today when life is going well for them. Ask them to specify how this day looks and what they are doing from early morning until late evening, the positive feelings they are experiencing, and what positive thoughts they are having.

APPLICATION 76. CREATE A FIVE-YEAR PLAN

Invite clients to look beyond the present to a time five years in the future. Ask them to take a large sheet of paper and divide it into sections. On the left, a vertical axis is drawn, and clients write down relevant domains in their life: work, family, friends, hobbies, money, etc. A horizontal axis is drawn at the top, divided in segments starting at six months and proceeding to one year, two years, and three, four, and five years (from left to right).

Ask clients to start with where they want to be in five years with respect to the life domains written on the vertical axis and to write their thoughts down for each domain under the five-year heading. Then ask them questions such as, "If you want to be there in five years, how far do you have to be in four or three years?" "What should you have achieved by then?" "And in two years?" "In one year?" "In six months?" "What can you start with right now?" Invite them to write down all their answers. The five-year plan helps clients to formulate realistic goals and to write them down in a timetable. This clarifies which steps they can take to maximize the chances that they will have achieved their goals in five years.

APPLICATION 77. VISUALIZE THE PREFERRED FUTURE

Invite clients to visualize their preferred future for a couple of weeks. Ask them to each day or night focus on different domains within the scene, such as their personal life, relationships, work, or study, to prevent reduction of the effectiveness of the visioning. Research has shown that repeated visualization of the preferred future, as in the "best possible self" application (number 67), enhances optimism, and that this optimism continues even after the intervention period is over (Meevissen et al., 2011).

APPLICATION 78. VISUALIZE THE NEXT SIGNS OF PROGRESS

Invite clients to visualize the next signs of progress, ensuring them that they are on the right track in reaching their goal. What would constitute progress? How would they/others notice that things are moving in the right direction? What else would they notice that is better of different?

APPLICATION 79. WRITE A EULOGY

A eulogy (from εὐλογία, *eulogia*, Classical Greek for "praise") is a speech or written document in praise of a person or thing, especially one who recently died or retired. It can also be used as an act of endearment. How would you like to be remembered when you die or retire?

Covey (1989) used a similar technique. He suggested that one of the seven habits of highly effective people is to begin with the end in mind. This means that people have a clear picture of their destination. If people know their destination, it becomes easier to discern how far they already are and to know that the steps they have taken are in the right direction.

A way to begin with the end in mind is to imagine that you are present at your own funeral or cremation in three years' time. Ask yourself, "What do I want my family, relatives, friends, and colleagues to say about how I made a positive difference in their lives?"

APPLICATION 80. IMAGINE AN ANNIVERSARY

Invite clients to choose three people who are dear to them, people who love them and whom they love. Ask them to imagine that they have an anniversary ten years later (for example, they have been married for twenty years or have been working for the same organization for fifteen years). Ask them to imagine that at this party these three people all gave a short speech. What do your clients want those three people to say about them? This is not about what they think they would say, but what they would like them to say.

This application is based on Covey's (1989) habits of highly effective people (see above).

APPLICATION 81. IMAGINE WINNING A PRIZE

It is nice to ask team members a variation of the previous application. Say to the team, "Suppose I meet you at the airport, and you tell me that you are going on a trip to collect a prize because you have become the best team in the world (or continent). You know that when you receive a prize, there always has to be a speech. So what are you going to say in that speech about how you work together as the best team? What are you going to say about how you managed that? What obstacles did you face, and how did you overcome them? And finally, whom are you going to thank?"

APPLICATION 82. VISIT AN IMAGINARY SHOP

There is an old Dutch rhyme that starts with "In de winkel van Sinkel is alles te koop. Hoeden en petten en damescorsetten [In the shop of Mr. Sinkel everything is for sale. Hats and berets and ladies corsets]."

Say to clients that in this fictitious shop, they can buy anything they want—for example, a pound of courage, a lion that protects them when they are doing difficult things, or scales where they first weigh the requests of others before they say yes or no. Invite clients to visit this imaginary shop, look around for a while, and then choose one or more things that may help them to achieve their goal or solve a problem. There is no need to pay anything, and they can always exchange things if they don't think they are useful or nice. What is special about the store is that they may also leave something behind they no longer need, such as a sack filled with perfectionism—perhaps other customers will find this useful. Invite them to use their new purchases and pay attention to whether and how these items help them to get closer to their goal.

IMAGINARY SHOP

A supervisee said she suffered from fear of exams. Because this was getting in in the way of passing her exams, she asked for help from her supervisor. The supervisor invited her to visit the imaginary shop. After looking around for a while, she chose three things: a beautiful white embroidered pillow on which she could lay her head when feeling tired, a black panther to walk ahead of her when she entered the scary forest of exams, and a little angel to sit on her right shoulder and compliment her on what she was doing (as opposed to the little devil on her left shoulder who criticized her). She chose not to leave anything behind in the store.

At home, she tried out her purchases by visualizing how the white pillow, the black panther, and the little angel on her right shoulder helped her during the upcoming exam. Later on, she used the visualization of her purchases while going to the exam and passed it.

Personal Growth

PP focuses on opportunities for growth and development. Personal growth is about the idea of progressive development: You see yourself as growing and open to new experiences and opportunities. More about the *growth mindset* can be found in Chapter 6. Personal growth can also take the form of *post-traumatic growth* after traumatic experiences (Bannink, 2014b; Tedeschi & Calhoun, 2004).

Invite clients to answer these questions to work on their personal growth:

- In what ways can they accept themselves, and in what ways not?
- What are theirstrengths and skills? How did they grow in these areas? How do they use them now?
- With whom are their most cherished relationships? How do they support them? How do these people on their turn support the clients?
- What would they like to improve in their life?
- What would they like to achieve? In what way will this make the world a better place?

People quickly get used to new material possessions, which make them happy for just a while. They would better off spending their time and money on collecting experiences, such as enjoying cosy dinners, making trips, going to concerts, or learning new things. Therefore, invite clients to think about how they will gather experiences instead of things.

Invite clients to find a hobby. This is important for everyone, but seems especially true if people are over forty (Dijksterhuis, 2015). Invite clients to find out what suits them, what they find rewarding, and what they can learn from. Or invite them to start a collection. It has been shown that people who are collecting things are happier than people without a collection.

APPLICATION 86. DEVELOP A POSITIVE ADDICTION

The key to building new healthy habits is to continuously repeat a specific behavior. Aristotle (1998) stated that we are what we repeatedly do. Excellence is therefore not a behavior, but a habit.

Habits are behaviors that have become automatic at any given time; they are elicited by a cue from the environment rather than by consciously thinking about it. When we think of habits, we mostly think of negative ones: biting our nails, procrastinating, or eating sweets. But we have good habits too: jogging or brushing our teeth. It is useful to not only break unhealthy habits and negative addictions, but also to develop healthy habits and *positive addictions*.

Invite clients to think about which positive addiction they would like to develop. Examples are going for a walk each day, doing something nice for another person or animal, or doing a mindfulness exercise each day.

WHO MADE YOU SMILE AGAIN?

It does not matter who hurt you or broke you down. What matters is who made you smile again.

Posttraumatic Growth

In recent years, there has been growing interest in the awareness that people can not only successfully cope with adversity and show resilience but also grow as a person. This is called posttraumatic growth (PTG). Growth can be experienced in increased spiritual awareness, increased self-knowledge, increased awareness of one's own strength, and a stronger sense of connection with others (Bohlmeijer & Bannink, 2013). It has been found that optimism, adaptive coping styles, and social support all promote posttraumatic growth, and that people who experience posttraumatic growth experience fewer depressive symptoms and more well-being.

Tedeschi and Calhoun (2006) developed the *Posttraumatic Growth Inventory*, an instrument for assessing positive outcomes reported by persons who went through traumatic experiences. This twenty-one-item scale includes the factors of New Possibilities, Relating to Others, Personal Strength, Spiritual Change, and Appreciation of Life. Women tend to report more benefits than do men, and persons who went through traumatic experiences report more positive change than do persons who have not. The Posttraumatic Growth Inventory is partially related to optimism and extraversion. The scale appears to have utility in determining how successful individuals are, when coping with the aftermath of trauma, in reconstructing or strengthening their perceptions of self, others, and the meaning of events.

Tedeschi and Calhoun (2004) offered some important caveats on PTG:

- PTG occurs in the context of suffering and significant psychological struggle, and a focus on this growth should not come at the expense of empathy for the pain and suffering of trauma survivors.
- For most trauma survivors, PTG and (symptoms of) PTSD will coexist, and the growth emerges from the struggle with coping, not from the trauma itself.
- Trauma is not necessary for growth; individuals can mature and develop in meaningful ways without experiencing tragedy or trauma.
- Trauma is not good in any way; life crises, loss, and trauma are seen as undesirable.
- PTG is neither universal nor inevitable. Although a majority of individuals experiencing a wide array of highly challenging life circumstances experience posttraumatic growth, there are also a significant number of people who experience little or no growth in their struggle with trauma, and this outcome is quite acceptable.

Talking about traumatic experiences can be a useful first step. Telling the story—sometimes for the first time—to an empathetic and accepting person (such as a therapist) may provide relief. Fear or shame may be reduced, and people may realize that they are not guilty of what happened but rather were a victim. The label "victim" may indeed be helpful in the beginning but in the long run can make people feel passive, depressed, anxious, or hopeless.

Beginning to see oneself as a "survivor" after some time is often more useful. You may ask clients, "How did you manage to survive during and after the traumatic experience(s)? How were you able to deal with the effects of these experiences? What helps you during the most difficult moments, if only a little?" These solution-focused questions help to shift the attention to other aspects of their story—to their strengths and resources. The questions create positive emotions, such as feeling satisfaction and pride in the way they survived and dealt with the traumatic experiences.

Clients who have gone through terrible events may see themselves as a *victim* or as a *survivor* (or even *thriver*). If they see themselves as a victim, it will be more difficult for them to play an active role in shaping their life. Clients were unable to do anything about what happened to them, and they expect that they cannot change much about the way the rest of their life pans out. They probably feel powerless and feel that they have lost control. However, when clients see themselves as survivors, the possibility of a more active role becomes apparent. It offers them the opportunity to organize and take control of their life, despite what they have experienced. This initiates a spiral of positivity and more control. I (Bannink, 2014b) have described my model of *posttraumatic success*, incorporating the 3Rs: Recovery, Resilience, and enRichment (posttraumatic growth). Kuiper and Bannink (2012, 2016) stated that in helping children and their families with traumatic experiences, the focus should be not only on risk factors, but first and foremost on protective and resilience factors.

APPLICATION 87. CHOOSE THE ROLE OF VICTIM OR SURVIVOR

There is a saying: *This is the first day of the rest of your life.* The following four-step application can help clients to find out which role they want to play in the rest of their lives, that of *victim* or *survivor* (or *thriver*).

1. How would they like to see their life in a month's time? The same people and circumstances are still present, but they feel a little less influenced by what they have experienced.
2. If they think about their answer to the previous question—that is, their goal in a month's time—how will they then think and feel, and how will they behave in order to reach their goal if they see themselves as a victim?
3. Invite them to answer the same question, but now from the perspective of a survivor (or even of a thriver).
4. What differences do they notice? What will they be doing differently? Which role is the most helpful to them?

Dolan (1998) stated that overcoming the immediate effects of abuse, loss, or other trauma and viewing oneself as a survivor rather than as a victim are helpful steps but are ultimately not sufficient to help people fully regain the ability to live a life that is as compelling, joyous, and fulfilling as it used to be. People who remain at the survivor stage see life through the window of their survivorhood rather than enjoying the more immediate and unobstructed vision of the world around them that they previously held. All experiences are evaluated in terms of how they resemble, differ from, mitigate, or compound the effects of past events. This diminishes their ability to fully experience and enjoy life and is responsible for the flatness and depression reported by many people who categorize themselves as survivors. In this vein, a third position may be added to the exercise: the position of a *thriver*. This position signifies that the trauma doesn't define the person any longer and has just become one part of who he or she is.

APPLICATION 88. WRITE FOUR RESOLVING LETTERS

Invite clients to follow the advice of Dolan (1998) and write four resolving letters after negative events:

1. The first letter includes all the unresolved feelings that clients have toward someone or something that happened to them.
2. The second letter is the response that clients fear, this being either a response from the perpetrator or someone who has bad intentions toward them.
3. The third letter is the letter clients hope they will get. It includes the acknowledgement the clients seek, and in the case of an attacker, it also includes an apology. Letter three should be written straight after letter two in order not to deepen the trauma but to ease it.
4. The fourth letter can be written at such a time as clients feel like it and represents the hope they have for a better future—a future in which the trauma is genuinely in the past and clients have gone beyond surviving it and have become *thrivers*.

APPLICATION 89. SHOW YOURSELF RESPECT

Invite clients to use the following tips from Furman (1998) for resilience and posttraumatic growth:

- Respect yourself for the many ways you have overcome difficulties.
- Consider the adverse events as experiences that have played a role in the development of your positive qualities.
- Pay attention to resources in and outside yourself, because there are probably a lot more than you think.
- Be proud of your progress and success and notice small signs that tell you that you are on the right track.
- Keep paying attention to what you want from life and the future. Sometimes wishes come true, but no wind helps a ship without a destination.
- Believe that you are entitled to a good future. The more difficult your past has been, the more you have earned a good future.
- Have compassion for others and for yourself.

APPLICATION 90. PLAY THE WHAT-IF GAME

A unique feature of resilience is that people can cultivate their resilience, independent of misfortune or fortune. They can even play the *what-if game*. This means that clients first imagine that something negative happens and then imagine what they would do to cope with this situation as well as possible and which resilience factors they would use (Grotberg, 1995).

APPLICATION 91. ASK ABOUT A DIFFICULT CHILDHOOD

Our past is a story we can tell ourselves in many different ways. By paying attention to methods that have helped us survive, we can start respecting ourselves and reminisce about our difficult past with feelings of pride rather than regret (Furman, 1998). Most people can view their past—including even the most extreme suffering—as a source of strength rather than of weakness. It is said that *it is never too late to have a happy childhood*. Invite clients who had a difficult childhood to answer the following three questions related to their experiences:

1. What helped you survive your difficult childhood?
2. What have you learned?
3. In what ways have you managed in later life to have the kinds of experiences that you were deprived of as a child?

APPLICATION 92. WRITE, READ, AND BURN

Another way in which writing may be helpful is to invite clients who are plagued by obsessive or depressive thoughts to write, read, and burn what they have written, as illustrated in the following case (Shazer, 1985).

A client who was obsessed with her ex-partner months after breaking off the relationship felt guilty and kept asking herself what she had done wrong. The thoughts had even grown into nightmares. After normalizing the problem, the therapist gave the client the following suggestion in order for her to move on with her life. At the same time every day, she was to retire to a comfortable place for at least an hour and no more than an hour and a half. During that time, she had to focus and, on all odd-numbered days, write down all her good and bad memories of her ex-partner. She had to keep writing the entire time, even if it meant that she ended up writing some things down more than once. On even-numbered days, she had to read her notes from the previous day and burn them. If the unwanted thoughts came to her at times other than during the scheduled hour, she had to tell herself, "I have other things to do now, and I will think about it when the scheduled hour has arrived," or she had to make a note to remind herself to think about it at the scheduled time. After just a few days, the thoughts had largely disappeared.

APPLICATION 93. THINK OF A RITUAL

Invite clients to think of a ritual; it can be one that is done just once or one that is repeated. Rituals are seen in many cultures; think of the ceremonies associated with weddings and funerals. These rites are designed to help with making the transition into the next phase in life. There are two types of rituals: (1) the one-time ritual people do to get past a (traumatic) experience and (2) the ritual people do more often and which becomes a habit, meant to prevent problems and to obtain stability and connection after a (traumatic) experience or change. The one-time ritual is specific, temporary, and helps because it invites people to become active instead of worrying. Usually in therapy, one works with a symbol that is related to the event, such as a picture or a piece of the car after the accident. In the ritual, the picture or piece of the car may be burnt, thrown away, or buried.

It is also helpful to invite clients to develop rituals that they can repeat.

These kinds of rituals can be carried out alone or with others and aim to connect people in a positive way. One example is to keep a diary or to go for a walk with someone every evening before going to sleep.

APPLICATION 94. DEVELOP A SHARED RITUAL

Invite clients to think of something they often did with another person. Maybe they went to the movies together every week, read a book aloud, took a walk, or massaged their partner. Given the circumstances in their present life, what new ritual can they think of to carry out for the next month? Ask clients to enact their plan with another person. Ask them to evaluate after a month whether this ritual suits both of them. If not, ask them to adjust it so that it feels better, or to invent another ritual they can do together and evaluate again after one month.

THE SHATTERED VASE

The metaphor of the shattered vase is often used in therapy with trauma survivors. Posttraumatic growth involves the rebuilding of the shattered assumptive world. Imagine that one day you accidentally knock a treasured vase off its perch. It smashes into tiny pieces. What do you do? Do you try to put the vase back together as it was? Do you collect the pieces and drop them in the trash, considering the vase a total loss? Or do you pick up the beautiful colored pieces and use them to make something new—such as a colorful mosaic? When adversity strikes, people often feel that at least some part of them—be it their views of the world, their sense of themselves, their relationships—has been smashed. Those who try to put their lives back together exactly as they were remain fractured and vulnerable. But those who accept the breakage and build themselves anew become more resilient and open to new ways of living.

These changes do not necessarily mean that the person will be entirely free of the memories of what has happened to them, the grief they are experiencing, or other forms of distress. It might mean that they live their lives more meaningfully in light of what happened (Bannink, 2014b).

Optimism

Seligman (2002) shifted his attention from *learned helplessness* to *learned optimism*. He conducted research on the factors that lead people to perceive an event as positive or negative and their reasoning behind this. Pessimistic people attribute negative events particularly to stable, global, and internal factors. They say, "Things never go right with me" (stable), "I will never be happy again" (global), and "I am good for nothing" (internal). They attribute positive events to temporary, specific, and external factors. They say, "That was only luck, which had nothing to do with me" when something positive happens.

Optimistic people think in the opposite way. They attribute positive events to stable, global, and internal factors. If something positive happens, they believe that it does say something about them—for example, "I really am valuable." Optimists attribute negative events particularly to temporary, specific, and external factors. They might say, "I couldn't do anything about it because he threatened me." Thinking in a pessimistic way, especially about negative events, leads to hopelessness.

Optimism and pessimism are relatively stable personality traits, but they can be influenced by the way someone acts and by what he or she focuses on. Optimism contributes to more adaptive survival strategies, namely, more positive reappraisal, better coping abilities, and more use of positive distractions (hobbies and exercise). Scheier and Carver (1994) found that optimism is partly determined by genetic factors and partly by upbringing.

There exists a positive correlation between happiness and optimism. Optimism is affected by the way people behave and what they pay attention to. Happy people are more optimistic about their future and are healthier than pessimistic people (Seligman, 2002).

In recent years, research has also been conducted on the benefits of optimism for physical and mental health (Peters, Rius-Ottenheim & Giltay, 2013). They found a clear link between optimism and better physical health, and between optimism and psychological well-being. Optimistic people are more resilient in stressful situations and have a lower risk of developing psychological problems such as depression. Optimism is also associated with better academic outcomes and a successful career (Carver, Scheier, & Segerstrom, 2010). It is therefore not surprising that Einstein said that he would rather be an optimist and a fool than a pessimist who was right.

Again, there are some caveats: Optimism is not always positive for everyone, and pessimism is not always negative for everyone. Think of evading one's responsibility by attributing events solely to external factors and engaging in reckless behavior by thinking that success always has to do with you. There are also cultural differences: Applications for optimism, such as visualizing your best possible self (see Application 67), work better for people with a Western background than they do for those with an Asian background (Boehm, Lyubomirsky, & Sheldon, 2011).

APPLICATION 95. LEARN OPTIMISM

Seligman (2002) stated that optimism may be learned. Therefore, invite clients to engage in a training course to become more optimistic (Bannink, 2009, 2012, 2015a, 2015b, 2016):

1. Each evening, write a sentence about the *nicest event* of the day as if it were caused by something stable, global, and internal (because I am/can). *Example*: "Today I received a compliment from my boss. Stable: This has long been the case, because I've received earlier compliments from him. Global: Apparently I'm a good worker. Internal: I got that compliment because I am reliable and good at this type of assignment."
2. Every night, write a sentence about the *worst event* of today as if it were caused by something temporary, specific, and external (because X, then Y). *Example*: "Today I was late for the appointment with my dentist. Temporary: This is the only time I was late. Specific: Usually I arrive on

time for appointments; this is an exception. External: I arrived late because I was stuck in traffic; I couldn't help it."

APPLICATION 96. INCREASE OPTIMISM

If clients want to increase their optimism, invite them to answer the following questions:

- What have you achieved already?
- What has helped you so far?
- How can you do more of what works?
- What do you want to achieve?
- What is your next small step?
- Who can help?

APPLICATION 97. IMAGINE THE WORST-CASE SCENARIO

Invite very pessimistic or anxious client to imagine the *worst-case scenario* before an event takes place. Ask them what the worst thing is that could happen and then compare what actually happens to this scenario to see if it even comes close (most of the time it doesn't).

APPLICATION 98. IMAGINE THE BEST-CASE SCENARIO

As a counterpart to the worst-case scenario (see previous application), invite clients to imagine the *best-case scenario*. In *positive cognitive behavioral therapy* (Bannink, 2012), this is called the *upward arrow technique*. Ask clients to answer the following questions:

- What is the best thing that could happen to you?
- Supposing this happens, what difference will it make?
- What else will be different, and what will you be doing differently (or better)?

APPLICATION 99. CHOOSE THE ROLE OF PESSIMIST OR OPTIMIST

This is an application in four steps that invites clients to find out what role is best for them and what suits them the most: the role of pessimist or optimist.

1. How would they like their life to look in one month's time?
2. When they think about what they thought (or wrote) above—their goal in one month's time—what would they think and feel and how would they behave in order to achieve their goal if they were a pessimist?
3. And what would they think and feel and how would they behave if they were an optimist?
4. What differences do they notice? What role is most useful for them?

FIVE GOLDS

Matt Biondi was one of the United States hopefuls for multiple medals in the swimming pool at the Seoul Olympics in 1988. In the two-hundred-meter freestyle, he finished a creditable third. The next event was the one-hundred-meter butterfly. Having dominated the race all the way, he made an error of judgment on his final stroke and was beaten by an unknown swimmer from Surinam. There was much criticism leveled at Biondi; this was not the start to a conquest of seven gold medals that everybody expected, and many started to write him off.

There was one person who did not, however. Seligman had evidence that Biondi had what it would take to come back from these disappointments and achieve success. Seligman had previously run an assessment program with the swimming team. The objective was to assess how each of them would perform, especially when under pressure and after setbacks. Having tested each swimmer on an optimism-versus-pessimism scale as well as on their explanatory style (i.e., the reasons people give for things going wrong), Seligman created a set of circumstances that simulated defeat. Each swimmer was asked to put in one of their biggest efforts on their best event. Their coach, who was in on the experiment, timed them. On completion, the swimmers were told that their time was worse than the actual time they had achieved. The level of the "failure" was made sufficiently large to be disappointing but not so large as to be obviously wrong. After a rest period, the swimmers were asked to do the same event again, as fast as they could.

There was a difference between optimists and pessimists in their reactions to the "failure" and, more importantly, in how they performed in their repeat swim: Pessimists performed worse. Their times deteriorated, even to lower than in their "correct" first swim, some by as much as two seconds, the difference between coming in first and last. Optimists, on the other hand, either sustained their performance or went even faster, Biondi being one of them. This is why Seligman was confident Biondi would bounce back from the first two events, and he did, securing five golds to go along with his silver and bronze.

4

Relationships

Happiness depends on what you can give, not what you can get.

—MAHATMA GHANDI

This chapter is about *relationships*, because having relationships and social connections is one of the most important aspects of life. We are social animals that thrive on connection, love, intimacy, and a strong emotional and physical interaction with other humans. Building positive relationships with our parents, siblings, peers, and friends is important for spreading love and joy. Having strong relationships gives us support in difficult times. It has been found that the happiest people have intense and meaningful relationships.

By investing time and energy in establishing and strengthening relationships (and enjoying it along the way), people not only become happier but also increase their likelihood of living longer. It may be enjoyable to share problems with someone, but our relationships will be better when we share not only our troubles, but first and foremost our successes. This

118

is called *capitalization* and works even better if the other person responds in an active and constructive way. In this chapter, applications for use in partner relationships are described. It has also been found that friendships contribute to a happier, longer, and healthier life. Many more applications are described that can be used both in partner relationships and in relationships with friends, classmates, and colleagues.

Relationships

When talking about positive relationships, we mean having warm, trusting relationships with others; caring about their well-being; being empathic; experiencing affection and intimacy; and appreciating giving and taking between individuals. Positive relationships are, according to Ryff (1989), one of the dimensions of psychological well-being. Reis and Gable (2003) distinguished three themes in positive relationships: intimacy, affection, and fun. Intimacy has to do with our fundamental need for connectedness. Affection includes love, sexuality, and attentive behavior. Fun also contributes to positive relationships because it involves enjoyable experiences and sharing new things with others. Experiencing excitement, enthusiasm, and inspiration together contributes to satisfaction and passion in relationships (Aron, Norman, Aron, McKenna, & Heyman, 2000).

Seligman (2011) added relationships as the third pillar of his well-being theory. Having positive relationships—partner relationships, but also social relationships—offers the best guarantee for the peaks of life and the best antidote to its valleys. Happiness and experiencing satisfaction are nurtured by having positive relationships. Diener and Seligman (2002) stated that one of the best predictors of happiness is strong social relationships.

When Peterson, one of the founders of PP, was asked how he would describe PP in two words or less, his answer was, "Other people." Little of what is positive in life happens when you're on your own. Do you have someone you can call at four o'clock in the morning to tell your troubles to? If your answer is "yes," you will probably live longer than if your answer is "no." Isaacowitz, Vaillant, and Seligman (2003) discovered the following in the Grant Study (see Chapter 1): The ability to love and to be loved has the strongest relationship with subjective well-being at the age of eighty. The human capacity to engage in loving relationships is probably one of the strongest capacities we have.

APPLICATION 100. FIND STRENGTHS IN THE ENVIRONMENT

A criticism of PP is the fact that it focuses mainly on individual strengths and not on communal strengths. So focusing on strengths outside of clients is useful. Ask them, "Who and what are your resources? With whom do you have a positive relationship? Who and what contribute to the times when you are not functioning optimally? With whom do you have a negative relationship?" The answers to these questions can help clients can make a plan for personal growth.

It's nice to experience lots of positive emotions. Sharing good news and positive events is also nice, and it has other advantages too. Gable et al. (2004) found that discussing personal positive events with others creates more daily positive emotions and well-being—more than the impact of the positive events themselves. This effect became even larger when others responded in an active and constructive way (see below). Relationships in which partners shared positive events and the other person responded enthusiastically have been associated with higher well-being and more satisfaction in the relationship. These partners felt more connected and more loving toward each other. This is called *capitalization*: It may be enjoyable to share problems with someone, but your relationships will be better when you share not only your troubles, but first and foremost your successes. Moreover, sharing problems may even be harmful to yourself and your relationship, because asking for and receiving support means that apparently there is something you are not good at. This can affect your confidence, which in turn may have a negative impact on your relationship. Capitalizing on positive events provides two other advantages. First, you start to feel better when you share something positive, because you experience the positive emotions once more. Second, you remember the positive event better when you share it with another person. In this way, capitalization builds individual and social resources.

APPLICATION 101. CAPITALIZE ON POSITIVE EVENTS

Invite clients to choose someone they like (their partner or someone else) whom they see every day. Ask them to share—capitalize—for a period of one week (or longer if they like) one or more positive events each day. This application will be most effective if the other person reacts in an active and constructive way (see below).

WATER THE FLOWERS, NOT THE WEEDS

Peacock (2001) stated that after a seminar he gave to 250 executives, half of them bought a watering can. They put their watering cans in plain sight in their offices to remind themselves that they were gardeners and that their job was to water what was working well in their organizations and in their personal life.

Seligman (2011, p. 53) took watering the flowers even more literally: "I am a rose gardener. I spend a lot of time clearing away underbrush and then weeding. Weeds get in the way of roses; weeds are a disabling condition. But if you want to have roses, it's not nearly enough to clear and weed. You have to amend the soil with peat moss, plant a good rose, water it, and feed it nutrients. You have to supply the enabling conditions for flourishing."

Love

According to Fredrickson (2009, 2013, p. 10), love is the most frequent positive emotion (see Chapter 2). She called love "our supreme emotion." Love is that micro-moment of warmth and connection that you share with another living being. It is our supreme emotion that makes us come most fully alive and feel most fully human. It is perhaps the most essential emotional experience for thriving and health. Love can encompass all other positive emotions such as joy, hope, pride, or thankfulness. When these feelings occur in a safe, intimate relationship, we call it love. If you just met someone, there's probably much interest and humor. If you get to know each other better, there is probably the joy of your new relationship and hope for a good future together. As the relationship deepens, there may be gratitude and satisfaction. Love increases the oxytocin level in the body, and oxytocin deepens relationships, mutual trust, and intimacy. And this is needed for the survival of the human species, because oxytocin ensures that partners stay together to raise their children.

Love also increases empathy and altruism, not only for the beloved person, but also for a larger circle of people. In other words, love follows the same logic of all other positive emotions: It broadens the attention and builds relationships, resilience, and health.

There exists a positive relationship between happiness and love. Married people report more happiness than unmarried people or people who are divorced.

According to Fredrickson (2013), love is a momentary upwelling of three tightly interwoven events:

1. Sharing one or more positive emotions between yourself and another
2. Synchrony between yours and the other person's biochemistry and behaviors
3. Joint motivation to invest in each other's well-being that brings mutual care

Fredrickson called this *positivity resonance*. Partners who regularly spend time together doing new and exciting things provide a large number of shared micro-moments of positivity resonance.

Lewicki and Wiethoff (2000, p. 87) described the concepts of *trust*, *trust development*, and *trust repair*. They stated that mutual trust is the glue that links people together. Their definition of trust is "an individual's belief in, and willingness to act on the basis of, the words, actions, and decisions of another." In their view, sharing a common goal is one of the best ways to build mutual trust.

Susskind and Cruikshank (1987) argued that it is unrealistic to ask clients to trust each other; trust must be earned. The overriding consideration of each client to trust the other is reciprocity: "Why should I keep my promise if the other doesn't?" Mutual trust can only be built, using small steps, if clients behave accordingly.

The *game theory* (Neumann & Morgenstern, 1944) deals extensively with this topic using the famous *prisoners' dilemma*. This is a standard example of a game analyzed in game theory that shows why two "rational" individuals might not cooperate, even if it appears that it is in their best interest to do so.

THE PRISONERS' DILEMMA

Two members of a criminal gang are arrested and imprisoned. Each prisoner is in solitary confinement with no means of communicating with the other. The prosecutors lack sufficient evidence to convict the pair on the principal charge. They hope to get both sentenced to a year in prison on a lesser charge. Simultaneously, the prosecutors offer each prisoner a bargain. Each prisoner is given the opportunity either to betray the other by testifying that the other committed the crime or to cooperate with the other by remaining silent. The offer is:

- If A and B each betray the other, each of them will serve two years in prison.
- If A betrays B but B remains silent, A will be set free and B will serve three years in prison (and vice versa).
- If A and B both remain silent, both of them will serve one year in prison (on the lesser charge).

It is implied that the prisoners will have no opportunity to reward or punish their partner other than the prison sentences they get and that their decision will not affect their reputation in the future. Because betraying a partner offers a greater reward than cooperating with him, all purely rational self-interested prisoners would betray the other, and so the only possible outcome for two purely rational prisoners is for them to betray each other. The interesting part of this result is that pursuing individual reward logically leads both of the prisoners to betray, when they would get a better reward if they both kept silent. In reality, humans display a systemic bias toward cooperative behavior in this and similar games, much more so than predicted by simple models of "rational" self-interested action.

I (Bannink, 2008b, 2010b) have described the game theory and its value for conflict management as well as the role of oxytocin in a greater sense of mutual trust.

APPLICATION 102. EXPERIENCE (MORE) LOVE

If clients want to experience (more) love and see that the glass is half full rather than half empty, invite them to do one or more of the following:

- Read about love and discuss it with others.
- Spend time with a family member and share how much appreciation they have for him or her.
- Spend time with their best friend and do something fun together.
- Spend time with a (grand)child and enjoy feeding the ducks or reading a story.
- Spend time alone quietly in a special place and think of all the people who love them.

APPLICATION 103. USE HONEYMOON TALK

Discussing the strengths and resources of yourself, your partner, and your relationship helps to strengthen the relationship. Invite clients to give each other compliments by describing each other's strengths, because it creates more mutual goodwill. *Honeymoon talk* (Elliot, 2012)—talking about the positive start of the relationship—is useful and also fun to do because it diverts attention from problems to previous successes.

Honeymoon talk can also be done with a team. Ask partners or team members to discuss:

- What do they think their partner/team member is good at?
- What do they like about their partner/team member?
- What do they appreciate about him or her?
- What is it about their partner/team member that makes them proud of them?
- What strengths do they see in their partner/team member?
- What strengths do they see in their relationship?
- How did they meet? What did they find special about their partner/ team member?

Gable and colleagues (2004) found that how people celebrate is more predictive of strong relationships than how people fight. Partners may tell each other about a victory, a triumph, or good things that have happened to them. How people respond can either build relationships or undermine them. There are four ways of responding, of which only the first helps in building positive relationships (see below). Every time someone you care about tells you about something good that happened to you, listen carefully and respond actively and constructively. The person may be asking to relive the event with you; the more time he or she spends reliving, the better. Seligman (2011, p. 51) stated:

Once you start doing it, other people like you better, spend more time with you, and they share more of the intimate details of their lives. You feel better about yourself, and all this strengthens the skill of active, constructive responding.

1. *Active and constructive*: Verbal: "That's great, congratulations! I know how important this is to you." Nonverbal: maintaining eye contact, displays of positive emotions such as smiling or laughing.
2. *Passive and constructive*: Verbal: "That's good news." Nonverbal: little to no emotional expression.
3. *Active and destructive*: Verbal: "That sounds like a lot of responsibility to take on. Are you going to spend even fewer nights at home now?" Nonverbal: displays of negative emotions such as frowning or crying.
4. *Passive and destructive*: Verbal: "What's for dinner?" Nonverbal: little to no eye contact, turning away, leaving the room.

APPLICATION 104. RESPOND IN AN ACTIVE-CONSTRUCTIVE WAY

Invite clients to do this application for *active-constructive responding*. Ask them to respond with a manner of genuine happiness, excitement, and active questioning to their partner when he or she shares good news. This allows their partner to reexperience the pleasure of the event and builds a stronger, more positive relationship between them.

APPLICATION 105. PRACTICE ACTIVE LISTENING

Invite clients to practice active listening by asking their partner how he or she is doing with the intention of taking the time to listen and react actively. They can also practice this spontaneously when someone wants to talk to them.

APPLICATION 106. CELEBRATE RELATIONSHIPS

Previously it was stated that a strong predictor of a good relationship is how people celebrate their relationship. So invite clients to check how they actually celebrate their relationship with their partner. Do they spend a holiday together, have a nice dinner, or go on some other adventure? Ask them to find things they do or can do with some regularity, and ask them to compliment each other on their relationship successes.

APPLICATION 107. PLAN A STRENGTHS DATE

Planning a *strengths date* is a great way to enhance a relationship and to increase positive emotions for clients and their partners through understanding, recognizing, and celebrating one another's character strengths. To plan a strengths date, first invite clients and their partners to complete the VIA Inventory of Character Strengths (see Chapter 1) so they know each other's top five signature strengths from this measure. Invite them to take as many of their signature strengths as they see fit and sculpt an activity together that taps into the individual strengths of both of them.

APPLICATION 108. OBSERVE WHAT THE OTHER PERSON IS DOING THAT IS HELPFUL

This is a solution-focused application used in couple's therapy (Bannink, 2010a; 2012). Invite both clients to notice what their partner is doing that is helpful in building a better relationship. Ask them to write down those moments and discuss them at the end of the week, with each other or with their therapist. Paying attention to the things people see their partner do that are helpful has a better effect on the relationship than paying attention to the things they see their partner do that are not helpful.

Friendship

Research shows that friendships also contribute to happiness and health. Sometimes we quarrel with friends, we feel envy, or we gossip about each other. Why, then, are friends important? It is because they can make us laugh when we are feeling down. Because they raise their glass with us when we have good news. And because friends play a major role in our best memories. Diener and Seligman (2002) compared the happiest people with the unhappiest people and found that the first group was very social and had the strongest relationships (note: this is correlational, not causal). Having good relationships was even a prerequisite to feeling happy.

Happiness appears to be contagious. If a friend of ours is happy, we are more likely to be happy too. Research at Harvard Medical School by Fowler and Christakis (2008) among 5,000 people shows that the happiness of a person extends within his or her social group and even to people he or she does not know personally ("three degrees of separation") and that this could last for one year. Sadness turns out to be less contagious: If you have a friend who is happy, the likelihood that you are happy increases 15 percent; if you have a friend who is unhappy, your chances of also being unhappy increase only 7 percent.

With friends, we talk more often about what we really think is important, and women especially look for social support—mostly with other women—when they are worried or struggling. This may explain why men's health deteriorates more through stress than women's health. Daily social support also contributes to optimism: We are more satisfied with life and have less risk of depression. We are more capable of seeing difficulties as challenges and mountains as molehills.

Our physical health also improves by having friends. We keep on exercising longer when we perceive social support. The memory of people who lack social support deteriorates earlier, and social support leads to less depression and suicide. People lacking social support are more likely to have higher blood pressure and other risk factors for heart disease. Moreover, they give up earlier on attempts to improve their situation when stressed or ill. Friendships ensure that we live longer: Women with breast cancer who had a good friend lived longer than women who had not. There is also a meta-analysis of 148 studies showing that people with strong social relationships were 50 percent less likely to die prematurely (Holt-Lunstad, Smith, & Layton (2010).

However, how social support is perceived or received has different consequences. Perceived social support is great; think of how happy people who have experienced a disaster can be with the help that is offered. Received social support, by contrast, is not always regarded as pleasant.

Sometimes people receive social support that they have not asked for. It is not only important to offer support, but also to do so at a moment in time and in a way that the other(s) will indeed perceive this as support. Therefore, it is sometimes better not to give advice and only validate clients' feelings.

APPLICATION 109. SPEND QUALITY TIME WITH FRIENDS

Positive relationships are important. To help or encourage clients to spend quality time with friends, invite them to answer these questions:

- When did you last really catch up with your friends?
- When was the last time you engaged in activities with your friends?
- When was the last time you did something for your friends?
- What might help you to set aside more time for paying attention to your friends?
- What could you do to have (more) friends?

APPLICATION 110. REFLECT ON SOCIAL INTERACTIONS

Invite clients to review their entire day each night for a few weeks and call to mind the three longest social interactions they had that day. Ask them to consider how true each of the following two statements is for them:

1. During these social interactions, I felt "in tune" with the person(s) around me.
2. During these social interactions, I felt close to the person(s) around me.

Ask them to rate the truth of these two statements on a scale from 1 to 7, where 1 equals "not at all true" and 7 equals "very true." They may record their responses anywhere—for instance, in a notebook or computer. As the weeks progress, they can see whether their well-being rises in step with their increased attention to social connections.

WHAT YOU GIVE IS WHAT YOU GET

Pioneers in the United States in the 1850s received free grants of land in the West if they were prepared to do the necessary work to make them livable. A family living on the East Coast undertook the long trip over the course of several months, finally arriving in the middle of the continent. They stopped near a stream to feed their animals and children and met an old farmer who had been living there for many years. They asked him, "What is it like in this region? Is it a good place to plant our seeds, to build our farm and raise our children? How are the people here? Are they good? Are they cooperative?"

The farmer replied, "What were the people like in the East where you came from?" The head of the family replied, "Oh, they were awful and not at all cooperative!" The old farmer said, "I am sorry to inform you that it is exactly like that here. It would be better to continue your voyage and look elsewhere for your new home."

Then another family arrived, and they had also traveled a long time coming from the East. By chance they stopped at the same stream, fed their animals and children, and met the same old farmer. Like the first family, they asked, "What is it like in this area? Is it a good place to plant our seeds, build our farm and raise our children? How are the people here?" The farmer replied, "What were the people like in the East?" And this family replied, "Oh, they were very kind, very helpful and cooperative." The old farmer said, "It is exactly like that here. My dear neighbors, welcome to your new land!" (Peacock, 2001).

APPLICATION 111. CREATE LOVING CONNECTIONS

Invite clients to seek out at least three opportunities to connect with others each day—with warmth, respect, and goodwill. Opportunities may spring up at home, at work, or in their neighborhood or community. Invite clients to be open toward others, offering their attention and creating a sense of safety through eye contact, conversation, or, when appropriate, touch. Ask them to share their lighthearted thoughts and feelings and stay present as the other person shares theirs. Ask them to afterward reflect lightly on whether that interchange led them to feel positive resonance, even to a small degree. Creating the intention to seek out and create more micro-moments of loving connection can be another tool for elevating their health and well-being.

APPLICATION 112. ENSURE CONNECTIONS AT WORK OR SCHOOL

Invite clients to take a look at their work or school environment. What part of their work are they doing with others? How much time do they spend working on connections with their colleagues or classmates? Do they make enough eye contact? Do they listen enough?

Positivity resonance can also be found in the workplace and in schools. How can clients ensure (even more) micro-moments of connection? Which new rituals or habits can they create to feel more connection in the workplace or at school? And how will they notice that their investment is successful?

APPLICATION 113. CREATE COMPASSION IN DAILY LIFE

Fredrickson (2013) described the following application, which she uses herself. Invite clients to look for opportunities to build their capacity to connect with others compassionately. Ask them to take in the faces and body postures of others; these need not be people with whom they are currently interacting. Mere passers-by are good targets for informal practice. Ask them to look for nonverbal signs, however small, of their suffering, any clue that this other person is carrying some burden (because, according to Fredrickson, everybody carries some burden). Then ask them to lightly let their heart and mind reflect on that source of pain for a moment and extend a simple wish for the person's release from pain and suffering by silently saying one or more of the following classic phrases:

- May your difficulties (misfortune, pain) fade away.
- May you find peace (ease, strength).
- May your burdens be lifted.

Ask them to experiment with new phrasings until they find a phrase or two that truly move them. Shifting their stream of attention is not a magical trick that whisks away all suffering from this other person. It is simply to condition their own heart to be more open and concerned about the pains and predicaments others inevitably face. Put differently, although their focus is on other people, the person who is most changed by this application is the client himself.

APPLICATION 114. EAT TOGETHER

Invite clients to eat together at least once a day together (with their partner, family, or friends). Ask them to ensure positive communication by sharing how they spent their day, evaluating pleasant events, making appointments, and looking forward to the coming days.

Wansink and Kleef (2014) found that eating together strengthens our connections and benefits our health and weight, because we are more at ease and take more time to eat instead of eating thoughtlessly, as happens when we watch TV at the same time.

APPLICATION 115. PERFORM ACTS OF KINDNESS

Lyubomirsky, Sheldon, and Schkade (2005) found that performing acts of kindness produces the single most reliable momentary increase in well-being of any PP exercises tested. Research shows that this will result in an increase in well-being, especially if people perform the five acts of kindness all in one day.

Invite clients to set themselves the goal of performing five new acts of kindness in a single day (they should not do them every day, since this may become boring and less effective) over six weeks. Ask them to aim for actions that really make a difference and come at some cost to them, such as donating blood, helping a neighbor with their yardwork, or figuring out a better way that their ailing father might manage his chronic pain. Ask them to be both creative and thoughtful and assess what those around them might need most. Ask them to make it a point to carry them all out on a single day. At the end of the day, invite them to notice the good feelings that come with increasing their kindness. For lasting impact, ask them to make their kindness day a recurring ritual and be creative each week. Ask them to find new ways to make a positive difference in the lives of others and try it for a few months to observe the difference it makes.

APPLICATION 116. COUNT ACTS OF KINDNESS

Invite clients to keep track of how many acts of kindness they perform on a daily basis. These can be simple things like helping someone cross the street, giving an extra compliment, or have a conversation with a stranger. Otake, Shimai, Tanaka-Matsumi, Otsui, and Fredrickson (2006) found that people feel happier and more grateful if they do this application for one week.

APPLICATION 117. DO SOMETHING NEW

Besides performing acts of kindness, doing something new also ensures more well-being (Buchanan & Bardi, 2010). Invite clients to now and then think of something new to do in order to broaden their interest and gain new experiences.

APPLICATION 118. FOCUS LESS ON YOURSELF

People who are too focused on themselves are less healthy and feel lonelier and less happy than those who think of others. Invite clients to help other people and make those people and themselves happier.

APPLICATION 119. GIVE SOMETHING YOU LIKE

Sometimes it turns out to be a good thing to be more focused on yourself. If you want to give a present to someone, you might think that this gift should be something that the recipient likes. But research shows that when you give an item that says something about you as a giver, this evokes more connection between the recipient and you (Aknin & Human, 2015). So invite clients to give as presents a book they love or a CD with music they are moved by.

APPLICATION 120. DO SOMETHING UNEXPECTEDLY POSITIVE

Invite clients to do something unexpectedly positive for another person each day and ask them to observe what happens to their mood. Ask them to step out of their comfort zone each day and watch the difference it makes for themselves and their relationships.

APPLICATION 121. SURPRISE SOMEONE

Sometimes clients are stuck in negative patterns with other people. The predictable way in which they react can be disrupted if they do something different (Bannink, 2012).

One way of doing this is by doing the *surprise task*, a playful way to challenge a person's fixed ideas. It is agreed with clients that they will do something (either subtle or highly noticeable) to surprise the other person in a positive way. What that might be is left to each client. The other person may then guess what the surprise was, and they can talk about it together at the end of the day or the week or at the next therapy session. Children and adolescents in particular take great pleasure in these surprise tasks, but the application can also be used with friends, in the classroom, or with a team.

APPLICATION 122. CREATE POSITIVE PARANOIA

This is an alternative to the previous application. Invite clients, such as team members or classmates, to secretly come together with another person as a pair and find a way to do something positive for someone else (family, group, class, or team). At the end of one week, the recipients guess which positive things all the pairs have been doing. The funny thing is that they often guess wrong.

APPLICATION 123. GIVE COMPLIMENTS

There are different types of compliments. A *direct compliment* is a positive evaluation or reaction by the therapist in response to the client. It can be about something the client has said, done, or made or about his appearance. A compliment can also be about the client's strengths or resources: "You must be a really caring mother to . . . . Please tell me more." Or "You must be a very determined person. Please tell me more about this determination of yours."

An *indirect compliment* is a question that implies something positive about the client. These questions invite the client to tell a success story about herself: "How did you do this?" "How were you able to . . . ?" or "Where did you get this great idea?"

Indirect complimenting is preferable to direct complimenting because its questioning format leads clients to discover and state their own strengths and resources.

Many clients accept compliments easily; others downplay or even reject them. But remember that the first goal in giving compliments is for clients to notice their positive changes, strengths, and resources. It is not necessary for them to openly accept the compliments. Also invite clients to give more compliments to others.

APPLICATION 124. USE POSITIVE REINFORCEMENT

Invite clients who would like to change the behavior of someone else to come up with three positive reinforcers of the desired behavior. What exactly is the behavior they would like to be different, and which positive reinforcers might they use? Invite clients to consistently apply these three reinforcers over the course of one week and vary their use. They can think of complimenting the other person when they see that person doing something they appreciate, or they can give a small present when the other person has helped them in any way. Ask them to observe the difference in behavior of the other person at the end of the week and how their relationship changes.

WHAT WE CAN LEARN FROM GEESE

As each goose flaps its wings, it creates an uplift for the bird following. By flying in a V- formation, the flock has 71% greater flying range than if the bird flew alone. Lesson one is that people who share a common direction and sense of community can get where they are going more quickly and easily because they are traveling in the slipstream of one another.

Whenever a goose falls out of formation, it feels the resistance of trying to fly alone and quickly gets back into formation. Lesson two is that we stay in formation with those who are headed where we want to go when we are willing to accept their help as well as give ours to others who are looking for support.

When the lead goose gets tired, another goose flies at the point position. It pays to take turns doing the hard tasks and share the leadership. Like geese, we are dependent on each other's skills and capabilities; no person is right to lead in all circumstances and at all times. Lesson three is that leaders need to let go at times, and others must feel comfortable in stepping forward.

When a goose becomes ill or wounded, two geese follow it down to help protect it. They stay with it until it is able to fly again or dies. Then they set off with another formation or catch up with their flock. Lesson four is that we stand by each other in difficult times as well as when we are strong.

The geese honk from behind to encourage those up front to keep up their speed. Lesson five is to make sure our honking from behind is encouragement and not something else. Production is much greater in groups where there is encouragement (Bannink, 2014a).

APPLICATION 125. COMMUNICATE RESPECTFULLY

The following four steps may help clients to respond respectfully and constructively if they suffer because of the behavior of another person and would like the other person to change that behavior:

1. Identify the specific behavior without judgment.
2. Express their emotion (use labeling).
3. Link the emotion to their needs.
4. Request what could enrich their life.

APPLICATION 126. FIND CONNECTEDNESS

Research shows that feeling connected to others brings more happiness. Below are some suggestions to start or renew relationships. It has been shown that when people have five or more friends (outside their family), the chances are 50 percent higher that they will describe themselves as happy. Maybe these people can help to achieve desired changes. Invite clients to start or renew their relationships by doing one or more of the following suggestions:

- Think about a way to restore a relationship with a friend they have neglected lately or have lost.
- Write a card, letter, or email to a friend and do not procrastinate.
- Call someone and do not procrastinate.
- Go and do something where they can meet new people.
- Make an appointment with one or more relatives or friends to do something together every week: have dinner together, do sports, or play a game.
- Start a chat with a stranger.
- Volunteer at an organization that provides assistance to people or animals.

APPLICATION 127. FIND SUPPORTERS

Invite clients—both children and adults—to answer the following questions:

- Who are your main supporters?
- How do they support you?
- What positive things would they say about you if I asked them?
- How do/did you support the people who support you?

APPLICATION 128. MAKE AN ACCORDION WITH COMPLIMENTS

Invite clients and their family, or team members, to write their name at the top of a piece of paper and to pass this paper on to the person beside them. Everyone writes on the piece of paper what strengths they see in the person whose name is on top of the paper and then passes the paper to their neighbor. At the end, the paper arrives back at the person whose name is on top of the paper, full of compliments. The paper can be folded like an accordion after each compliment so that no one can see the others' comments.

APPLICATION 129. CREATE AN APPRECIATION WALL

Invite clients or team members to create an *appreciation wall*. This can be done in about 30 minutes and is a fun way for them to give feedback to each other. It helps them capture one another's strengths, creates energy, and promotes relationships and trust. Ask them to create the wall as follows:

- Hang a large sheet of paper on the wall and write in large letters at the top of the sheet, "What we appreciate about each other."
- Divide the paper into squares for all those present.
- Invite everyone to grab a pen and to write in each box (or use Post-its) what they appreciate about each other.
- Observe together what everyone has written down and ask them to share some explanations and examples. It may be interesting to talk about some of the appreciative statements.
- The team leader may ask questions: "Who wrote this compliment?" "How did you notice this person has this strength?" "What do you appreciate about it?" "What makes it valuable for you to have a colleague who does this?" Often the responses are enthusiastic. Compli-

menting people directly and accepting compliments can sometimes be awkward, but with this application, it usually is very easy and pleasant.

APPLICATION 130. CREATE A COMPLIMENT BOX

Invite clients to make a *compliment box* during therapy with couples, children, families, or groups. At the end of the session, each participant puts a note with a compliment for each one of the others in the box. These notes are read aloud during the next session. The compliments may be given anonymously or signed.

A variation of the compliment box is the *success box* (see Application 175 in Chapter 6).

APPLICATION 131. GOSSIP POSITIVELY

Reduce negativity and promote an upward spiral of positivity by inviting clients to gossip in a positive way. In positive gossip, the strengths and successes of others are discussed. By conveying a positive image of the other person, the relationship between them and others is influenced implicitly. Clients can think about others in a positive way: What do they appreciate about them? What strengths do they see? How do these other people contribute to their family or team? Also, invite them to gossip positively about the other person, whether or not in the presence of that third person.

A nice way to gossip positively is to first create groups of three people. Person A and person B gossip for two minutes about person C, as if C is not there and cannot hear them. C sits with his or her back to A and B and is not allowed to respond. After two minutes, person B and person C gossip for two minutes about A, and finally C and A gossip for two minutes about person B. Positive gossip is always appreciated; people often hear things about themselves that are new, moving, or surprising.

APPLICATION 132. USE HAPPINESS DETECTIVES

Invite a small group of children in the classroom or a few team members to become *happiness detectives*. Their mission is to track down all the things they see others doing that lead to the class becoming a place with more happiness and well-being. All the ideas that fulfill this mission are first listed. After a week, the small group gets together again and shares their discoveries. Subsequently, there are regular monthly gatherings at which the group discusses what they have seen in the class or team, which promotes well-being. Such a group can be formed as support for a certain child, student, or team member who has difficulties, or it can simply be started up without any specific reason. The groups can swap around from time to time.

Teachers who launched *happiness detectives* at school found that the children who spent some time being happiness detectives acquired better social skills and more self-confidence and showed better cooperative behavior in the class (Young, 2009). Happiness detectives can also be used in group therapy and in organizations.

APPLICATION 133. START WITH A POSITIVE OPENING

Always start a meeting or session with a positive opening. Invite clients to briefly mention a recent (small) success or an accomplishment of which they are proud. Another form is a short round with the question, "What are you pleased about (at work or at home)?" This increases the chances that the rest of the meeting or session will develop in a positive atmosphere. Invite clients not to make judgments; everything is accepted and is given compliments by the others. Also, the application "List three blessings" (number 30) can be done at the start of the meeting by inviting everyone to voice (three) things that have gone well since the last meeting.

APPLICATION 134. HOLD POSITIVE MEETINGS

Many people find meetings a waste of time. Holding meetings in a positive way (Bannink, 2010c) can change this. Always start a meeting with the end: As the chairperson, ask at the start of the meeting what needs to happen for the participants to consider the meeting successful. This gives a good indication of their desired outcome. Next ask if there are any questions participants want to address during the meeting, because asking this at the end of the meeting almost always ensures that the meetings take more time than scheduled. Try holding meetings standing up (meetings will surely be shorter) or sitting on top of the tables, and notice what difference that makes.

APPLICATION 135. SAY "YES, AND" INSTEAD OF "YES, BUT"

The use of "yes, but" is extraordinarily common. "Yes, but . . ." is frequently heard within teams and organizations. In reality, "yes, but" is simply a form of "no, because . . . ," just not expressed in a direct way: "Yes, but . . . I see that differently." "Of course you are right, but . . ." With "yes, but," you always nibble a little bit off of whatever was said before. In a therapy session with a client or in a meeting, a "yes, but" makes for negative emotions in no time at all, and the conversation will lead nowhere. A downward spiral will ensue. In fact, few people actually recognize the subtle negative influence of using "but."

The main reason to use "yes, and" instead of "yes, but" is that it influences dialogue in a positive manner. When using "and" instead of "but," there is a sense of inclusion and acceptance instead of exclusion and negation (see Table 4.1). It is a worthwhile exercise to become more comfortable with the ability to switch from one to the other. It is more beneficial to use "yes, and" to generate positive emotions. Now new possibilities emerge and an upward spiral of positivity is created. It stimulates cooperation with others and resilience within teams.

TABLE 4.1
Differences between "Yes, but" and "Yes, and."

"Yes, but"	"Yes, and"
Excludes or dismisses what precedes it	Expands and includes what precedes it
Negates, discounts, or cancels what precedes it	Acknowledges what precedes it
Is often perceived as pejorative	Is often perceived as neutral or positive
Suggests the first issue is subordinate to the second	Suggests there are two equal issues to be addressed

APPLICATION 136. CONTROL ANGER

Is expressing anger always the right thing to do? Research shows that the expression of anger actually increases rather than decreases that anger (Bushman, Baumeister, & Stack, 1999). This may lead to emotional and social harm, poorer relationships, and more stress. It is better to mentally distance yourself from the source of the anger. Counting to ten or just walking away can do this. Invite clients to look again at whether the other person gave them real reason to be so angry or aggressive, because upon reflection it is often not so bad.

Lieberman et al. (2007) found that labeling—finding a calm way to put feelings into words by simply putting the name to the emotion—decreases the response in the amygdala, the portion of the brain that handles fear, panic, and other strong emotions; anger decreases and become less intense. What lights up instead is the right ventrolateral prefrontal cortex, the part of the brain that controls impulses. The same strategy of putting feelings into words is seen in *mindfulness meditation* practice. This involves a regular practice of stepping back and observing the flow of experience. So invite clients to start labeling their emotions instead of just venting them, because venting anger feeds the flame.

APPLICATION 137. APOLOGIZE

Something people feel guilty about or are ashamed of may haunt them for years, resulting in stress and poorer health. Invite clients who are haunted by guilt or shame to apologize for what they did, because this will probably be helpful. Lazare (2004) studied the effects of more than a thousand apologies. Usually the receiver reacts positively to the apology, provided it is sincere and well presented. Invite clients to recognize what they did wrong, and ask them not to exculpate themselves when giving an explanation for what happened. Ask them to show genuine repentance and to inquire what they can do to make it right.

APPLICATION 138. FORGIVE

Being angry at someone has a negative impact on our immune system. When we experience negative emotions, the level of cortisol (stress hormone) rises. So invite clients to learn to forgive someone in order for anger to disappear and negative emotions to be reduced. Forgiveness is one of the character strengths within the fifth virtue of self-control (see Table 1.1).

BECAUSE OF THE MERCY YOU SHOWED

A popular hagiographic story circulated about the Sufi Al-Shibli, who lived in Baghdad. After his death, a friend saw him in a dream and asked him what God had done with him, to which Al-Shibli replied that God had placed him before Him and asked him if he knew why He had forgiven him his sins. Al-Shibli had suggested that it might be because of the good works he had done, the prayers he had performed, his fasting and pilgrimages, his having associated with pious people, or his journeying in search of knowledge. God replied that these were not the reasons. Al-Shibli had answered that these were the only things he could think of that might have saved him, to which God said, "Do you remember when you were walking in the lanes of Baghdad and you found a small cat made weak by the cold creeping from wall to wall because of the great cold and ice, and out of pity you took it and put it inside a fur you were wearing so as to protect it from the pains of the cold? Because of the mercy you showed the cat, I have had mercy on you" (Kugle, 2007).

5

Meaning

Being happy doesn't mean that everything is perfect. It means that you've decided to look beyond the imperfections.

—FRIEDRICH NIETZSCHE

This chapter is about *meaning*, because finding meaning and a purpose for being on this earth is important to living a life of happiness and fulfillment. There is an actual meaning to our life beyond the pursuit of pleasure and material wealth. To understand the greater impact of our work and why we chose to pursuit that work will help us enjoy our tasks more and become more satisfied and happier. Living a meaningful life is not only about us, but also about something larger than us, about altruism, about caring for others: To what extent do we have the feeling of being part of and contributing to a greater whole?

The larger this is, the more meaning we will probably experience. At the root of the meaningful life is knowing what our signature strengths are and deploying those in the service of something we believe is larger than we are, such as nature or religion.

We know that having multiple sources of meaning in life protects against a lack of purpose. Emmons (1997) stated that, empirically, people's lives usually draw significance from multiple sources, including family and love, work, religion, and various personal projects. Meaning reflects the basic human need for order, relationships, and hope and should be actively sought, co-created, and nurtured.

According to Baumeister and Vohs (2005), the quest for meaning can be understood in terms of four main needs: (1) the need for purpose, (2) the need for values, (3) the need for a sense of efficacy, and (4) the need for a basis of self-worth. In this chapter, these four requirements are described as well as the virtue *transcendence*, which encompasses the five character strengths that forge connections to the larger universe and provide meaning (see Table 1.1): (1) appreciation of beauty, (2) gratitude, (3) hope, (4) humor and playfulness, and (5) spirituality.

Meaning

In postmodern thought, agency, choice, and possibility are emphasized. The central importance of meaning for the quality and continuing emergence of human life is recognized. The essence of meaning is *connection*. The meaningful life consists in belonging to and serving something that we believe is bigger than we are. Increases in the level of meaning enhance positive satisfaction and fulfillment. At the root of the meaningful life is knowing what our signature strengths are and deploying those in the service of something we believe is worthwhile.

Meaning in life is a prerequisite for well-being and resilience. It can be found internally in our thoughts and reflections and externally in our connectedness with others, charity, and spirituality. Research shows a strong positive correlation between meaning and psychological well-being (Zika & Chamberlain, 1992).

Frankl (1963) had an optimistic view of meaning: He argued that life has meaning under all circumstances, even in intense suffering from which there is no escape. Frankl said of his stay in a German concentration camp during the Second World War that a prisoner who no longer believed in the future—his future—was doomed. He described an incident where he staggered along in a row of prisoners on his way to the work area, in the cold and without food. He forced himself to think about something else. Suddenly he saw himself standing on the stage of an auditorium where he was giving a lecture about the psychology of the camp system. In this way he succeeded in lifting himself above the suffering of the moment and was able to view the torment as if it already were in the past. His focus on the future saved him for that moment. This vision of the future even became reality, as after the war he conducted many successful lecture tours.

According to Frankl, the challenge for every person is to find unique meaning. Life itself does not provide meaning but offers everyone the opportunity to determine what is meaningful to them. Finding meaning becomes more difficult when there is no future perspective. Why are you alive then? A link has been found between a lack of meaning and addiction problems (Crumbaugh, 1971).

LOGOTHERAPY

In his logotherapy, Frankl (1963, p. 96) explained that the meaning in suffering is resilience itself: The trick is to handle the challenges that we face in life as well as possible. Rather than power or pleasure, logotherapy is founded upon the belief that it is the striving to find meaning in one's life that is the primary, most powerful motivating and driving force in humans.

The pessimist resembles a man who observes with fear and sadness that his wall calendar, from which he daily tears a sheet, grows thinner with each passing day. On the other hand, the person who attacks the problems of life actively is like a man who removes each successive leaf from his calendar and files it neatly and carefully away with its predecessors, after first having jotted down a few diary notes on the back. He can reflect with pride and joy on all the richness set down in these notes, on all the life he has already lived to the fullest. What will it matter to him if he notices that he is growing old? Has he any reason to envy the young people whom he sees or wax nostalgic over his own lost youth? What reason has he to envy a young person? For the possibilities that a young person has, the future which is in store for him?

"No, thank you," he will think. "Instead of possibilities, I have realities in my past, not only the reality of work done and of love loved, but of sufferings bravely suffered. These sufferings are even the things of which I am most proud, although these are things which cannot inspire envy."

Seligman and colleagues (2005) conducted a large-scale randomized controlled trial study of the effects of the application of character strengths in a new way (see Application 140). In this (online) study, participants were first given feedback on their character strengths and then instructed to put one of these strengths to use in a new way. Both immediately after using the application and as much as six months later, the participants scored higher on well-being and were less depressed than participants who did not do the exercise. Mongrain and Anselmo-Matthews (2012) replicated the study. They compared this new use of character strengths with the describing of childhood memories and found that the strengths application had a significantly stronger effect on the well-being of the participants than writing about childhood memories. Six months later, this effect was still present. With regard to depression, however, they found that this application had no effect.

APPLICATION 139. FIND MEANING

Invite clients to think about the following questions:

- What holds deep meaning for you?
- Do you know why?
- How can you apply your "why" to your personal and professional life?

APPLICATION 140. USE CHARACTER STRENGTHS IN A NEW WAY

Deploying your character strengths ensures lasting well-being, according to Seligman and colleagues (2005). Invite clients to fill out the VIA survey of character strengths, or ask them to look at the twenty-four character strengths in Table 1.1. Then invite them to make time to use one or several of their character strengths in a new way, at work, at home, or in their spare time. If one of their character strengths is creativity, you may ask them to write a story or a poem. Ask them afterward how they felt before, during, and after the activity. Was it a challenge or easy? Did the time pass quickly (was there *flow*)? Would they like to repeat the activity? Remember that the positivity, which arises when people find new ways to use character strengths, is permanent.

APPLICATION 141. FIND MEANING AND PURPOSE

Having something meaningful to look forward to every day fulfills the human need to make a meaningful contribution to one's life and the lives of others. Invite clients to do something simple every day, such as expressing appreciation of others with a smile, a touch, or a compliment; donating to a charity; or just calling someone to say hello.

APPLICATION 142. FIND MEANING IN THE BEST, WORST, AND MOST ORDINARY EVENTS

Ask clients to find meaning each day, and the long-term benefits of the three best, the three worst, and the three most ordinary events in their life.

The focus on meaning began with the study of how meaning could help people cope with misfortune and bad events; up until that point, the focus of psychology had been predominantly on the negative. Although nowadays most of the models of well-being include a component of meaning (e.g., the PERMA model described earlier), evidence does demonstrate the important role of meaning in well-being and quality of life. Snyder and Lopez (2007) have proposed the formula "Happiness + Meaning = Well-Being," thereby assigning a more important role to meaning in a person's well-being. Also, according to Ryan and Huta (2009), a eudemonic perspective (the good life; see Chapter 3) of subjective well-being should have a greater focus on meaning and virtue. Wong (1998, 2014) stated that one cannot have a high quality of life if it is devoid of meaning and purpose. He proposed that meaning should be the overarching framework for well-being and mental health. Wong went on to define personal meaning as a socially and individually constructed system that endows life with personal significance. According to Wong, there are five components to this constructed system: affective, emotional, cognitive, relational, and personal. For individuals with a meaning mindset, the pursuit of well-being emphasizes meaning and virtue not just for oneself, but also for humanity. Even in the absence of positive affect and active engagement, one can still enjoy certain levels of well-being based on meaning, virtue, and spirituality. According to Haybron (2000) pleasure itself does not really matter, as it is merely a by-product that accompanies the achievement of what is truly worthwhile. In other words, pleasure is simply the icing on the cake. Chapter 3 described how Seligman concurs with this view.

TWO MOST IMPORTANT MOMENTS IN LIFE

It is said that two moments are most important in your life:

1. The moment you are born.
2. The moment you find out why.

APPLICATION 143. CROSS A RIVER

Surviving a traumatic experience is like crossing a river: While fending for yourself, you may develop new meaning for your life and skills that may help you in the future. Invite clients to think about a painful experience and answer the following questions:

- What did you learn from surviving this experience?
- What does it mean to you/others to have survived this experience?

- What strengths or talents did you draw on then or develop later to survive the experience?
- How can these strengths or talents be best used to your advantage now?

Besides the role that positive emotion plays in health and well-being, Wong (2014) stated that meaning contributes to effective coping and the reduction of stress through several pathways. First, adaptive attribution and explanation can contribute to hope and then success. Second, coping strategies such as acceptance and seeing the positive potential of negative events are important in dealing with situations beyond our control. Third, having a clear sense of meaning and purpose contributes to the will to live in extreme situations. And fourth, resources for dealing with stress can be cultivated in preventive coping. In summary, meaning provides two important things: It helps protect well-being through the use of effective coping, and it ensures more well-being by helping to find purpose and develop resources.

Wong (2014) found that meaning is related to both the presence of well-being and the absence of mental illness. Mascaro and Rosen (2008) found that a sense of meaning as measured by the *Personal Meaning Profile* (PMP; Wong, 1998) was negatively related to depressive symptoms, depression, and hopelessness and positively related to meaning, fulfillment, hope, and an internal locus of control. A Dutch translation of the PMP administered to cancer patients was found to have a positive correlation with psychological well-being and a negative correlation with distress (Jaarsma, Pool, Ranchor, & Sanderman, 2007). Although these studies are correlational, there are some perspectives as well as longitu-dinal studies that show that meaning can predict future well-being (Mascaro & Rosen, 2008).

The National Center on Addiction and Substance Abuse at Columbia University polled 1,987 teenagers and 504 parents. Bored teenagers are 50 percent more likely to smoke, drink, and use illegal drugs. The studies highlight that at the core of an addiction is a search for significant experiences, an escape from boredom, and a longing for the rush that comes from consuming the substance of choice. Addiction, it seems, is a pseudo-search for meaning, a replacement for having little or no compelling purpose in your life.

Wong (2014) stated that meaning should be part of any global measurement of well-being or quality in life. Also, intervention programs to reduce distress and improve the quality of life should incorporate meaning-enhancing exercises and activities.

APPLICATION 144. DESCRIBE HOW YOU WANT TO BE REMEMBERED

Invite clients to make a description of their life as they would like to be remembered by their (grand)children or a young child they care about. How has their life been meaningful? Ask them to review what they have written at a later date and see what they need to add to make the summary realistic. Then ask them to take a small step toward fully living their goals for themselves and to observe what difference that makes.

Four Basic Needs

As was stated at the beginning of this chapter, Baumeister and Vohs (2005) found that the quest for a meaningful life can be understood in terms of four main needs: (1) the need for purpose, (2) the need for values, (3) the need for a sense of efficacy, and (4) the need for a basis of self-worth. These four needs constitute patterns of motivation that guide how we make sense of our lives. People who satisfy all four needs are likely to report finding their lives to be very meaningful. In contrast, people who are unable to satisfy one or more needs are likely to report insufficient meaning. These four basic needs are described in detail below.

The Need for Purpose

The essence of the need for purpose is that present events draw meaning from their connection with future events. There are two types of purposes. One is to have a goal or goals: a concrete, desired but not yet real outcome. The person's present activities take on meaning as a way of transforming the current situation into the desired (future) one. The second type of purpose is fulfillment, which is a state of being rather than anything material. Life can be oriented toward an anticipated state of future fulfillment, such as living happily ever after, being in love, or going to heaven.

Purpose—a cognitive process that defines life goals and provides personal meaning—creates and sustains health and well-being (Kashdan & McKnight, 2009). It offers direction just as a compass does. It offers meaning through goal pursuit and goal attainment and is central to one's personality. Meaning does not always drive purpose; rather, meaning drives the development of purpose. Once purpose becomes developed, it drives meaning; they have a temporal, back-and-forth relationship.

Purpose and goals are not synonymous either. Simply having a goal will not necessarily indicate a purpose. Goals focus on a specific endpoint and serve to guide us toward that endpoint. Purpose provides a broader motivational component that stimulates goals and influences behavior. It motivates us to be goal-oriented.

WORKING TOWARD A GOAL

Happiness is different for each person, but one factor virtually guarantees its boost: working toward a goal. Lyubomirsky (2008) found that people who strive for something personally significant, whether it is learning a new craft, changing careers, or raising moral children, are far happier than those who do not have strong dreams or aspirations. Find a happy person, and you'll find a project. Pursuing a goal provides several benefits: greater feelings of purpose and control, increased self-esteem and confidence, greater structure and meaning, sharper planning and prioritizing skills, increased ability to cope with problems, and opportunities to engage with others.

A worthwhile goal should be personally meaningful and rewarding. It should be one an individual freely chooses rather than one that is imposed on him or her. For example, you are less likely to find lasting happiness being a doctor to please your parents than being an architect to please yourself. The goal should move an individual toward doing something (such as learning a new skill) rather than acquiring something that improves his circumstances (such as moving to a bigger house). People soon get used to improvements in their circumstances and no longer get the same degree of pleasure from them, whereas activity goals produce a steady inflow of positive feelings and experiences. Setting goals helps people channel their energy into action (Bannink, 2010a).

The Need for Values

Having values lends a sense of goodness or positivity to life and can justify certain courses of action. Values enable people to decide whether certain acts are right or wrong. In Frankl's discussion of the meaning of life (1963), he emphasized value as the main form of meaning.

Overholser (1994) stated that sometimes it becomes a challenge for therapists to shift the focus onto the bigger picture of life, values and virtues, instead of dwelling on clients' minor concerns, weekly stressors and common sources of worry. However, it is the therapist's job to keep the focus on bigger and more meaningful topics for discussion during therapy sessions.

Invite clients to answer the following questions:

1. How can you live (even more) in line with your values?
2. What could be (even) better if you made some changes in your life?

The Need for a Sense of Efficacy

A sense of efficacy is about the belief that one can make a difference. A life that has purpose and values but no efficacy is tragic, because one knows what is desirable but can do nothing with that knowledge. A lack of control may provoke a personal crisis with a negative impact on physical and mental health.

The Need for a Basis of Self-Worth

The last need, according to Baumeister and Vohs (2005), is the need for a basis of self-worth. This can be developed individually, such as finding ways of positively comparing oneself to others or finding reasons for believing that one is a good and worthy person. It can also be created collectively, such as when people draw meaningful self-esteem from belonging to some group or category of people that they regard as worthy.

Invite clients to think about the following:

1. Five things they like about themselves
2. Five things they do that add value to the world around them
3. Their proudest achievement in the last twelve months

Trancendence

In the classification of the six virtues and twenty-four character strengths (see Table 1.1), the virtue *transcendence* encompasses the five character strengths that forge connections to the larger universe and provide *meaning*: (1) appreciation of beauty, (2) gratitude, (3) hope, (4) humor and playfulness, and (5) spirituality. These five character strengths are described below.

Appreciation of Beauty

Appreciation of beauty consists of different types of goodness. People may, for example, appreciate physical beauty. This produces awe and wonder. People may also appreciate skill or talent (excellence). This is often energizing and makes people want to pursue their own goals; it produces admiration. Virtue or moral goodness makes the individual want to be better, makes him or her more loving, and produces feelings of elevation.

It sadly often takes a traumatic experience or significant loss for us to reappraise our priorities in life and appreciate what we have. Survivors of traumatic experiences have much to teach those who haven't experienced such traumas about how to live.

The idea that finding positive meaning in suffering has long-term emotional or coping benefits is not new. The Greek philosopher Epictetus (60–120 AD) wrote that people are less disturbed by things than by their views of those things. However, finding benefit following a loss or trauma and finding meaning appear to be distinct, uncorrelated processes. They unfold along different time courses. People who find meaning shortly after a loss appear to find more positive meanings and have better emotional adjustment than people who find meaning long after a loss. In contrast, finding benefit in a loss is associated with positive adjustment regardless of when benefits are found (Nolen-Hoeksema & Davis, 2005). Three benefits commonly reported are (1) experiencing that the event led to a growth in character, (2) a gain in perspective, and (3) a strengthening of relationships. Nolen-Hoeksema and Davis (2005) discovered a strong link between optimism and finding significance in life after a loss. People who have positive expectations—optimists—are actively committed to seeking ways of transforming bad times into good times. They actively search for positive ways to look at the situation. And the more they preoccupy themselves with that, the greater the chance that they will find something positive.

A focus on merely recovering from trauma or loss to a previous level of functioning misses the process of change that many people experience following a loss or trauma. Rather than expecting people to "get back to normal," we should look for ways that trauma or loss contributes to growth and higher levels of functioning: *posttraumatic success* (see Chapter 3; Bannink, 2014b).

APPLICATION 147. FIND A KERNEL OF POSITIVITY

In the saying *It is better to have loved and lost than never to have loved at all* nestles a kernel of positivity. However sad clients are, and however difficult life may be in the beginning, invite them to discover something positive in their situation. Perhaps there is something for which they can be grateful? Could something have been worse? What is it about their situation that prevents it from being even worse?

Research shows that it doesn't matter how small the positive aspect is, so long as people can eventually find something that is positive. This small aspect can be the seed they sow to harvest more positivity in the future.

APPLICATION 148. WRITE A RAINY DAY LETTER

When clients are most in need of comfort, it is often most difficult to remember or figure out what will help. The *Rainiy Day Letter* (Dolan, 1998) provides consolation when clients need it most. They can carry the letter with them wherever they are. It offers them wisdom from the person who knows them best: themselves. Invite clients to set aside some time when they are feeling calm and ask them to write this letter to themselves, including the following:

- A list of activities they find comforting
- The names and phone numbers of supportive friends or family members

- A reminder to themselves of their character strengths and virtues
- A list of their special talents, abilities, and interests
- A reminder to themselves of their hopes for the future
- Special advice to themselves or other messages that are important to them

Gratitude

Gratitude, thankfulness, or gratefulness is a feeling or attitude in acknowledgment of a benefit that one has received or will receive from a person who gave, or gives, to them spontaneously of his or her own free will. Maslow (1970, p. 137) studied individuals who achieve self-actualization, the final level of psychological development that can be achieved when all basic and mental needs are essentially fulfilled. He found that these people were capable of seeing the good things in life over and over again and of being grateful for them. They see joy and inspiration in everyday life, not only in special events. Maslow stated that expressing gratitude is essential for emotional health: "Life could be vastly improved if we could count our blessings as self-actualizing people do."

Gratitude has historically been a focus of several world religions and has been considered extensively by moral philosophers. With the advent of PP, gratitude has become a mainstream focus of psychological research. The study of gratitude has focused on the understanding of the short-term experience of the emotion of gratitude (*state gratitude*), individual differences in how frequently people feel gratitude (*trait gratitude*), and the relationship between these aspects. Gratitude is probably a considerable *protective factor* against the development of many psychological disorders such as PTSD.

Gratitude is distinct from *indebtedness*. While both emotions occur following help, indebtedness occurs when a person perceives that he or she is under an obligation to make some repayment or compensation for the aid. These emotions lead to different actions; indebtedness can motivate recipients of aid to avoid the person who has helped them, whereas gratitude can motivate recipients to seek out their benefactor and to improve their relationship with them.

Research on gratitude shows the following results. In an experimental comparison, people who kept gratitude journals on a weekly basis exercised more regularly, reported fewer physical symptoms, felt better about their lives as a whole, and were more optimistic about the upcoming week compared to those who recorded hassles or neutral life events (Emmons & McCullough, 2003). A related benefit was observed in the realm of personal goal attainment: Participants who kept gratitude lists were more likely to have made progress toward important personal goals (academic, interpersonal, and health-based) over a two-month period compared to subjects in the other groups.

A daily gratitude intervention (self-guided exercise) with young adults resulted in higher reported levels of the positive states of alertness, enthusiasm, determination, attentiveness, and energy compared to a focus on hassles or a downward social comparison (ways in which participants thought they were better off than others). There was no difference in the levels of unpleasant emotions reported in the three groups. Participants in the daily gratitude group were more likely to report having helped someone with a personal problem or having offered emotional support to another compared to the groups that focused on hassles or social comparison. (Emmons & McCullough, 2003).

In a sample of adults with neuromuscular disease, a twenty-one-day gratitude intervention resulted in more positive emotions for the participants. It also resulted in a greater sense of feeling connected to others, more optimistic ratings of one's life, and better sleep duration and sleep quality relative to a control group. People with an *attitude of gratitude* have lower levels of stress hormones in their blood (McCraty, Barrios-Choplin, Rozman, Atkinson, & Watkins, 1998), and the cardiovascular after-effects of negative emotions are negated (Branigan, Fredrickson, Mancuso, & Tugade, 2000). Also, children who practice grateful thinking have more positive attitudes toward school and their families (Froh, Sefick, & Emmons, 2008).

However, some caution is necessary when looking at the applications for gratitude: They are not always effective. They can even be harmful for people who feel depressed (Sin, Della Porta, & Lyubomirsky, 2011). Moderately depressed individuals may have deficits that prevent them from taking full advantage of some positive practices. Such individuals may benefit more from simple pleasant activities than from reflective ones. More research is needed to identify specific activities that are optimal for individuals within specific affective ranges.

Research on gratitude (cited in Seligman, 2002) shows the following results:

- Expressing gratitude has a short-term positive effect (several weeks) on happiness levels (up to a 25-percent increase. Those who are typically or habitually grateful are happier than those who aren't habitually grateful.

- People who noted the things they were grateful for on a weekly basis increased their happiness levels 25 percent over people who noted their complaints or were just asked to note any events that had occurred during the week.

- People who scored as severely depressed in a depression inventory were instructed to recall and list three blessings that happened each day for fifteen days. Ninety-four percent of them went from severely depressed to mildly to moderately depressed during that time (see Application 30).

APPLICATION 149. KEEP A GRATITUDE JOURNAL

Invite clients to buy a handsome blank book to be their *gratitude journal*. Ask them to describe the things for which they are grateful each day. For example, my daughter just brought me a cup of tea as I sit at my computer, writing this book.

A more elaborate application than Application 40 consists of the following. Beyond simply listing good things in their life, an effective strategy is to describe *why* each good thing happened, in a few sentences. Doing so draws clients' eye to the precursors of good events. For this application not to become boring, they may choose to do it a few days a week instead of every day.

APPLICATION 150. MAKE A GRATITUDE VISIT

Invite clients to close their eyes and recall the face of someone still alive who years ago did something or said something that changed their life for the better—someone whom they never properly thanked; someone it is possible for them to meet face-to-face. Then ask them to write a letter of gratitude to this person and deliver it in person. The letter should be concrete and about 300 words; clients should be specific about what the person did for them and how it affected their lives. Ask them to let this person know what they are doing now and mention how they often remember what he or she did. Once clients have written the testimonial, ask them to call the person and tell them they would like to visit, but ask them to be vague about the purpose of the meeting; this application is much more fun when it is a surprise. When they meet the person, have them read the letter aloud to the recipient and take their time reading the letter. Have them notice the reaction of the person listening to the words as well as their own reaction. If the receiver interrupts as they read, ask clients to say that they really want the other person to listen until they are done. After clients have read the letter (every word), ask them to discuss the content with the other person and share their feelings for each other. Research shows that people will be happier and less depressed one month from now. There is a nice YouTube film showing this experiment in gratitude at http://www.youtube.com/watch?v=oHv6vTKD6lg.

The gratitude visit can also be done in a *virtual* way. This may be of particular use if the person is no longer alive or lives too far away to actually visit.

APPLICATION 151. WRITE A THANK-YOU NOTE

Invite clients to write a thank-you note, at least once a month—a greeting card, app, or email—to someone who has helped them with something.

Colleagues who are thanked for their help perform better at work than colleagues who do not receive a thank-you note.

APPLICATION 152. GIVE THANKS FOR THE ORDINARY AND THE EXTRAORDINARY

Invite clients to note, each morning after waking up, at least twenty things for which they are grateful. This may seem daunting, but once they get into the habit and find the right frame of mind, it will become easier. Here are examples of things they could appreciate: "I have hot and cold running water, I have a roof over my head, I have clean clothes, my kids are healthy, I am alive, I have friends." Ask them to experiment to discover what works best: writing down the appreciations, saying them out loud to their partner or a family member, or silently noting them to themselves. Invite them to do this activity for a week and notice what difference it makes. Then ask them to decide whether they would like to continue this habit.

APPLICATION 153. BE GRATEFUL IN FOUR STEPS

Miller (1995) described a cognitive behavioral program for gratitude in four steps. By following this program, clients may experience greater satisfaction and well-being. The four steps are as follows:

1. Focus on some of your nongrateful thoughts.
2. Then formulate some grateful thoughts instead.
3. Replace the nongrateful thoughts with the grateful thoughts.

4. Translate into action the inner positive feeling from the grateful thoughts: Do something with that good feeling.

APPLICATION 154. COUNT YOUR BLESSINGS

Invite clients to "count their blessings" just before they go to sleep. Ask them to think about everything that went well that day and what they are grateful for. They will probably sleep better and have nicer dreams. Also see Application 30.

WHAT ARE YOU GRATEFUL FOR?

I once walked through San Francisco, looking for a restaurant. My eye fell on a restaurant in the Bay Area named Gratitude. "What are you grateful for?" was written in large, luminous letters on the wall of the restaurant. It was really nice to just stop and think about this for a while as I looked for somewhere to eat.

There exists a positive relationship between gratitude and well-being. Gratitude has important implications for social functioning and well-being. It has three functions:

1. Gratitude acts as a barometer, because it keeps an eye on changes in social relations and provides greater well-being when someone does something good for another person.
2. Gratitude acts as a motivator, because it invites people to be more social.

3. Gratitude acts as a reinforcer, as it enlarges the chances of others doing good deeds in the future.

Research shows multiple evidence for the first and third function; the second hypothesis is still insufficiently researched (McCullough, Kilpatrick, Emmons, & Larson, 2001).

In order to increase well-being, a thank-you-therapy was designed to counteract materialism and negative emotions like envy, bitterness, depression, and disappointment. Application 153 describes a cognitive behavioral therapy program for gratitude.

Gratitude creates better relationships, including relationships with partners and children. Gable and colleagues (2004) found that when we share gratitude or appreciation, whether in words, gifts, or anything else that is positive, our relationships become stronger and more intimate. They could predict how long a relationship would last based on the degree of appreciation young people had for a Valentine's gift they received. Also new roommates became better friends when they were asked to express appreciation to each other.

GRATEFUL TO BE ABLE TO BE GRATEFUL

A client told her therapist that she had eventually succeeded in putting the rape behind her. She remarked at one point that she was "grateful to be able to be grateful" for surviving and being able to enjoy the good things in life again.

It is not hard to feel thankful when everything is going well in your life. But what about gratitude when everything goes wrong or if clients experience traumatic events? Do they still manage to be grateful? The Bible says people should be thankful in all circumstances, but is this realistic? And how can people do that? It turns out that counting your blessings despite difficult circumstances is a great human power. In that respect, there sometimes need to be contrasting circumstances for gratitude to happen, such as a harsh winter that allows people to be grateful for the first signs of spring or fasting that precedes enjoying a good meal. There may be gratitude for the difficult circumstances themselves, and gratitude for the way people handle the situation or for the sense of better times to come. Also, people can be grateful for what is still there after a loss, such as parents who are grateful that their children were unharmed after their home was destroyed by fire.

Reminding yourself regularly to be thankful is an important way of dealing with adversity and contributes in an important way to posttraumatic growth and resiliency. It increases positive emotions, meaning, and appreciation for life. Emmons and Shelton (2005) stated:

> Grateful individuals are not naively optimistic, nor are they under some illusion that suffering and pain are nonexistent. Rather, these persons have consciously taken control by choosing to extract benefits from adversity, with one of the major benefits being the perception of life as a gift. (p. 468)

APPLICATION 155. FIND BALANCE IN YOUR COMPLAINING

Life is not always easy, and sometimes complaining is all right. But people do not improve their well-being by complaining a lot. First invite clients to count the number of times per day they complain about adversity. Then ask them to look each day for the same number of things that they are grateful for to find a good balance.

APPLICATION 156. DWELL ON MORTALITY AND LOSS

Invite clients to think occasionally about death and loss. Ask them to dwell on their own mortality and that of their loved ones. Ask them to imagine that the beautiful and good things that happened in their lives never happened. Or ask them to refrain from doing—temporarily—something that they enjoy. The contrast with their real life will probably lead to more gratitude.

Hope

The third character strength involved in transcendence is *hope*: the belief that the future will be better than today (this belief is the same as in optimism) *and* the belief that an individual can influence this. Hope is strongly related to meaning because it is through self-reflections about our goals and the perceived progress toward those goals that we construct meaning.

Since the 1950s, physicians and psychologists have pointed to the role of hope in health and well-being. In his 1959 address to the American Psychiatric Association, Menninger suggested that the power of hope was an untapped source of strength and healing for patients. He defined hope as "a positive expectancy of goal attainment" and "an adventure, a going forward, a confident search" (Menninger, 1959, p. 484). Menninger stated that hope is an indispensable factor in psychiatric treatment and psychiatric education. The interest in hope in psychotherapy was initially aimed at reducing despair rather than increasing hopeful thoughts. Given the link between despair and suicide, A. T. Beck, Weissman, Lester, and Trexles (1974, p. 864) focused on combating hopelessness. Their definition of hopelessness was "a system of cognitive schemas whose common denomination is negative expectations about the future."

Snyder (1994, 2002) proposed a two-factor cognitive model of hope that similarly focuses on goal attainment. Snyder focuses not only on expectancies, but also on the motivation and planning that are necessary to attain goals. He defined hope as a positive emotional state that is based on an interactively derived sense of successful (a) agency and (b) pathways (planning to meet goals).

In order to reach goals, people must view themselves as being capable of generating workable routes to those goals. This process is called *pathway thinking*. It signifies one's perceived capabilities of generating workable routes to desired goals. The motivational component in hope theory is agency—the perceived capacity to use one's pathways to reach desired goals. *Agency thinking* reflects the self-referential thoughts about both starting to move along a pathway and continuing to progress along that pathway (e.g., "I can do this" or "I am not going to be stopped"). Agency thinking is important in all goal-directed thought, but it takes on special significance when we encounter impediments. During such instances of blockage, agency thinking helps us to apply the requisite motivation to the best alternative pathway. Hope has been shown to be applicable and to relate to performance in various domains, including the workplace (Youssef & Luthans, 2007).

These definitions tie hopeful thinking expressly to goals. By focusing on goal objects, we are able to respond effectively to our surrounding environment. Snyder and colleagues distinguished high-hope people from low-hope people. Compared to low-hope people, who tend to have vague and ambiguous goals, high-hope individuals are more likely to clearly conceptualize their goals (Snyder, Michael, & Cheavens, 1998).

In addition to setting goals, hope theory encourages people to set *stretch goals* (Snyder, 2002): goals that are difficult enough to be challenging but easy enough to be accomplished. Such goals encourage us not only to "patch up" problems but also to grow as individuals. For example, a stretch goal might be to increase well-being or connectedness instead of just resolving the problem. Continuously setting and meeting stretch goals is a way to move oneself toward a more positive, strengths-based stance. Hopeful thought reflects the belief that one can find pathways to desired goals and become motivated to use those pathways. Hope thus serves to drive emotions and well-being.

DESPAIR AND HOPE

According to Fredrickson (2009), there are two basic responses to hardship: despair and hope. In despair, negativity is multiplied. Fear and uncertainty may turn into stress, which can change into hopeless sadness or shame. Despair smothers all forms of positivity, and all possibilities for genuine connections with others are lost. Despair opens the gate to a downward spiral. Hope, however, is different. It is not the mirror reflection of despair. Hope acknowledges negativity with clear eyes and kindles further positivity, allowing an individual to connect with others. Hope opens the gateway to an upward spiral that empowers someone to bounce back from hardship and emerge even stronger and more resourceful than before.

APPLICATION 157. SEARCH FOR HOPE

According to the hope theory, three things are necessary to (re)gain hope. Invite clients to:

1. Find a destination (goal).
2. Design a mental roadmap.
3. Assume that they can achieve their goal and will find an alternative route in case of obstacles.

APPLICATION 158. ENHANCE HOPE

This is an application for professionals. Think of a personal problem, a concern or irritation. Invite a colleague to ask you problem-focused questions regarding this issue for about five minutes, such as, "What exactly is going on?" "How long has this been bothering you?" "How is this affecting you or others?" Then start the same conversation again, this time inviting the colleague to ask you solution-focused questions for five minutes, such as, "What do you want instead of the problem?" "What are your best hopes?" "What difference will that make?" "When is there already a glimpse of how you would like things to be?" Take a moment to notice the differences between the two conversations, and then switch roles.

The protection *hope* gives in coping with political turmoil, forced immigration, social injustice, and trauma has historically been exemplified by various spiritual models throughout human history, from Moses, Jesus, and Muhammad to Martin Luther King Jr. A study on post-9/11 mental health linked faith and perceived spiritual support with hope in American students with diverse religious beliefs, which was in turn associated with better mental health in these students with diverse beliefs (Ai, Cascio, Santangelo, & Evans-Campbell, 2005). Another research model demonstrated the importance of hope in the connection between positive coping due to religious beliefs and postoperative adjustment in American, predominantly Christian, cardiac patients (Affleck, Tennen, Croog, & Levine, 1987). The cross-cultural evidence implies that hope as a positive psychological virtue may be a universal resource for constructive adaptations and changes, which can also be enhanced in various spiritual beliefs.

Cognitive coping involves processing and comparing information, which may direct attention from the present trauma to alternatives. It may shift negative counterfactual rumination, which focuses on regret for not being able to avoid trauma, to a more positive orientation and to setting new physical and psychological goals for adapting to the new situation. Hope can be enhanced in clients by finding out what they are most excited about and then asking them to spend time with the most hopeful person(s) they know. Other ways to enhance hope are to tell clients stories about people in similar situations who have overcome hardship. One can also help clients identify and focus on the positive steps they have taken so far or help them to see the positive aspects of the situation. Explain to clients that focusing on what we want in life can in fact create the life we want.

APPLICATION 159. ASK QUESTIONS ABOUT HOPE

Solution-focused questions about hope and how hope can increase (Bannink, 2010a, 2015b) are:

- What are your best hopes? What difference will it make when your best hopes are met?
- What has kept your hope alive during this difficult situation/period?
- Supposing you had a bit more hope, how would your life be different?
- How would more hope help you reach your goal?
- What is the smallest change that could happen in your situation that would increase your hope?
- When did you feel (more) hopeful, and how did you manage that?
- What smell, color, song, or sound reminds you of hope?
- What rating do you give the situation on a scale of 10 to 0, where 10 equals "I am very hopeful" and 0 equals "I have no hope at all"?
- How is it that you are at that number and not lower?

- What will one point higher on the scale look like?
- How could you move up one point?
- What would someone who has (more) hope do in your situation?
- If you wanted your hope to increase by our next session, what would you do or what would you like me to do before we see each other again?
- What in our conversation today has given you more hope, even if only a little?
- What indicates that you are on the right track to solve this problem?
- Suppose the positive moments were to last longer. What difference will that make for you?
- What good things need to happen in your life to give you hope that you can leave behind the bad things that have happened?

APPLICATION 160. EXPERIMENT WITH HOPE

What works for one person may not work for another person, so invite clients to experiment with hope. It helps if there is room for humor, because laughter reduces stress and can put things in perspective. You can also ask clients to think of anything that reminds them of hope, such as a beautiful stone or a picture of better times, so that they can occasionally call it to mind or watch it.

APPLICATION 161. PREDICT THE NEXT DAY

Hope usually grows slowly. Invite clients to predict the next day and in doing this discover that there are exceptions to the problem and that they may have more control than they thought.

Ask them to think, every night, about what their next day will look like. Ask them to give a number for the next day on a scale of 10 to 0, where 10 stands for a very good day and 0 stands for the opposite. At the end of the next day, ask them to give a number for how the day went and to compare this with the number they predicted. Was their prediction correct? How did they know? Was the prediction not correct? What was different?

APPLICATION 162. ANSWER FOUR BASIC SOLUTION-FOCUSED QUESTIONS

Asking questions lies at the heart of solution-focused interviewing. Ask clients the four basic solution-focused questions (Bannink, 2010a, 2015b):

1. What are your best hopes?
2. What difference will achieving these make?
3. What works?
4. What will be the next signs of progress? What will be your next step?

APPLICATION 163. SEE HOPE AS A JOURNEY

Hope theory states that hope can be seen as a journey: People need a destination, a roadmap, and a vehicle (the idea that they can achieve their goal). Ask clients which part of the road they have already traveled and what their next steps might be to bring their destination closer. Ask them to determine where they would like to be in the future on a scale of 10 to 0, where 10 means they have reached their goal (destination) and 0 means the opposite. Where on the scale would they say they are today? How is it that they are at that number and not lower? What's working? What else? What skills and character strengths did they use? Also ask them what the next sign of progress would look like. What does a number higher on the scale look like? What will be different when they reach that number, and what will they do differently then? How will others react differently when they are there? And how much hope and confidence do they have that they can reach a higher number?

APPLICATION 164. FIND A GLIMMER OF HOPE

If clients want to find a glimmer of hope, even in a crisis situation, ask them the following solution-focused questions:

- What helped in the past, if only a little?
- How do you manage to deal with all that is happening and has happened?
- How do you manage to keep going?
- Could the situation be worse than it is? How is it not worse?
- What do people around you know that you do well, even in adversity?
- Suppose, in about ten years' time when you feel better, you look back on today. When you do this, what will you see that helped you?
- Supposing there is a solution, what difference will that make? What else will be different—and better?

A HOPEFUL DIAGNOSIS

A severely ill man was in the hospital. The doctors had given up any hope of a recovery. They were unable to ascertain what the man was suffering from. Fortunately, a doctor famous for his diagnostic skills was due to visit the hospital. The doctors said that maybe they could cure him if this famous doctor was able to diagnose him. When the doctor arrived, the man was almost dead. The doctor looked at him briefly, mumbled "moribundus" (Latin for dying), and walked over to the next patient. A few years later the man—who did not know a word of Latin—succeeded in finding the famous doctor. "I would like to thank you for your diagnosis. The doctors had said that if you were able to diagnose me, I would get better."

APPLICATION 165. OPEN A DOOR

Another intervention to cultivate more hope comes from Proyer, Ruch, and Buschor (2013). To promote hope, clients reflect on how a major loss tends to generate a vital opportunity, called "One door closes, one door opens."

With this intervention, first invite clients to remind themselves of something that has gone wrong in the past ("One door closes"). The next step is to invite them to think about the positive effects of this closed door ("One door opens"). Clients should not downplay the memory and are encouraged to develop a balanced view of what happened in the past.

An experiment with a control group showed that people who had done this intervention for three months reported enhanced life satisfaction compared to those in the control group (Hendrickx & Bormans, 2015).

APPLICATION 166. DEVELOP HOPE AT WORK

The good news is that hope can be developed. Hope allows for more individual initiatives and more motivation in employees. Start a new project with the joint formulation of a goal (destination) that everyone supports. Ask the above questions for enhancing hope. Think of ways to achieve the goal—for example, through a brainstorming session in which anything goes. Choose the most promising routes and find out where obstacles may occur. Together, think of ways to deal with those obstacles, thus increasing hope and confidence that these obstacles can be resolved. Finally, choose from the promising options the most appropriate (in terms of time, money, etc.) and go for it!

Humor and Playfulness

The relevance of humor and playfulness and the positive ways in which humans cope with stress in their daily lives seems to be self-evident. However, the ancient Greeks saw humor as a form of hostility where people laughed about the ugliness and disabilities of others, and therefore humor was considered undesired and cruel.

Among the earliest psychological contributions depicting the positive effects of humor was a paper on humor written by Freud (1928). Freud stated that humor enables us to gain perspective and relief from the emotions felt when we are disappointed. It involves the reinterpretation of failures as being of lesser importance or seriousness than we initially believed; humor is a good alleviator of emotional distress. From an evolutionary perspective, humor helps to avert the likelihood of violence between people and also enhances interactions within social groups.

Bonanno and Keltner (1997) found that bereaved persons who can smile and laugh as they speak about their deceased loved ones are judged to be more attractive and appealing than those who remain solemn. Laughter, smiling, and humor signify that mourners are ready to return to social interaction, making it easier for others to approach them. Humor is associated with positive changes in immune system functioning by reducing negative affect and/or increasing positive affect.

Playfulness also generates positive emotions. Why do kids play? They play because it just feels good to play. In playing, they try new things and learn from them, connect with others, make new friends, and strengthen their bodies. It broadens their attention and builds relationships, resilience, and health along the way.

APPLICATION 167. BUILD HIGH-QUALITY CONNECTIONS

Here are four ways for clients to build high-quality connections. Engaging with others in one or more of these ways transforms ordinary or corrosive interchanges with others into sources of positivity.

1. Be present, attentive, and affirming.
2. Support what the other person is doing. Enable the other person to succeed.

3. Trust the other person. Believe they can depend on this person to meet their expectations, and let it show.

4. Play. Allow time simply to goof off, with no particular outcomes in mind.

Spirituality

Spirituality may be seen as a way of seeing the world more deeply. People who see the world through a spiritual lens tend to experience several benefits, such as the ability to draw on whatever they hold as sacred as a reservoir of valuable resources throughout life's ups and downs. However, until recently, spirituality was an often-unwelcome topic of discussion in psychology. This has changed in the past quarter century. Seligman (2011) stated that after a half century of neglect, psychologists are again studying spirituality and religiosity in earnest, no longer able to ignore their importance to people of faith. Do you have an articulate philosophy of life, religious or secular, that locates your being in the larger universe? Does life have meaning for you by virtue of attachment to something larger than you are?

The term *spiritual* has changed from solely being a synonym for *religious* to a term echoing many of the themes emphasized in PP (e.g., caring, compassion, forgiveness, generosity, hope, gratitude, love, responsibility, and wisdom).

Until now, research has shown different results concerning the correlation between religion and well-being: On the one hand, research is showing that religion enhances well-being, while on the other hand research is showing that the two don't go well together. This might be the result of the extreme poverty of many religious people in developing countries.

There is now considerable evidence that a higher level of spirituality goes hand in hand with greater well-being, less mental illness, less substance abuse, and more stable marriages (Myers, 2000; Seligman, 2011). The literature also suggests that spiritual domains of experience may be influential to an individual's growth in the aftermath of stressful life events (Bannink, 2014b; Bray, 2009).

O'Hanlon (1999) described the *three Cs of spirituality* as sources of resilience:

1. *Connection* means moving beyond your little, isolated ego or personality into connection with something bigger, within or outside yourself.
2. *Compassion* means softening your attitude toward yourself or others by feeling with rather than being against yourself, others, or the world.
3. *Contribution* means being of unselfish service to others or the world.

APPLICATION 168. PRACTICE SPIRITUALITY

People who are involved in spirituality tend to be happier. They feel more connected to life on this earth and beyond (whatever it may be). From this perspective, people often feel that they have a specific role to play on earth. People do not have to be religious or belong to a church to be open to spirituality. Invite clients to see how they can practice spirituality.

APPLICATION 169. TAKE CARE OF YOUR BODY

The ancient Romans used to say *Mens sana in corpore sano*—"A healthy mind in a healthy body" is important. A healthy body is a temple for spiritual and emotional energy. Invite clients to pay attention to what they eat and drink, to take a walk or exercise, meditate or practice yoga, and see to it that they get enough sleep. Invite them to take good care of their body. They have only one!

THE SKY AT NIGHT

A man had been away for a long time. He had not really enjoyed his trip because he had missed the familiarity of his own home. When he finally started for home, his heart lifted. Unfortunately, tragedy had struck in his absence; his house had burned to the ground. All that remained was blackened ash and the smoky smell of his lost home.

"Why me?" he asked. "What did I do to deserve this?" But he soon realized that it was just one of those unfortunate life events. Such questions can only lead to pain and depression. They would not help him to deal with the loss, find a purposeful direction for the future, or take action—such as finding a place to sleep for the night.

A wave of sadness washed over him. For years, his homecomings had felt like returning to a beloved friend. But he knew it was acceptable to grieve for a loss, so he stayed mindful of his sadness until he felt like it was time to move on.

Next he found himself wishing it hadn't happened. If he had checked to ensure the cooking fire had been extinguished, his little home might still be there. "But it has been destroyed," he said. "That is the reality. Wishing for something that can't be changed can only result in more unhappiness and suffering."

As he focused on the remains of his house, he continued to be plagued with questions and doubts. Realizing this, he looked up. Twinkling stars dotted the sky, and a full moon smiled down benevolently. A sudden thought made him smile. "I may have lost my house, but now I have an uninterrupted view of the sky at night" (Burns, 2001).

6

Accomplishment

In order to succeed, people need a sense of self-efficacy, strung together with resilience to meet the inevitable obstacles and inequities of life.

—ALBERT BANDURA

This chapter is about *accomplishment*, because having goals and ambition in life is important too. We should make realistic goals that can be met, and just putting in the effort to achieving those goals can already give us a sense of satisfaction. When we finally achieve those goals, we will reach a sense of pride and fulfillment. Pursuing success, accomplishment, winning, achievement, and mastery for their own sake will help us to thrive and flourish.

Seligman (2011) added this fifth element to his well-being theory. Most of us are trying to achieve something—like writing successful books ☺—and we get to master things, even if this does not bring positive emotions, meaning, or positive relationships. It is called *the performing life*: a life devoted to performing, just for its own sake.

An important question is to what extent we should focus on problems and failures instead of on accomplishment and success. Appreciative inquiry (AI; see Chapter 1) reversed the prevailing *80-20 deficit rule*, which focuses 80 percent on what is wrong—impossibilities, (repairing) problems, and (reducing) errors—and 20 percent on what is right. AI uses what I call the *80-20 success rule*, with a focus of 80 percent on possibilities, successes, and progression and 20 percent on risks and what is wrong. *Solution-focused interviewing* (Bannink, 2010a, 2015b) also reverses this deficit rule, and this same approach is reflected in *positive supervision* (Bannink, 2015a).

We know that success is not possible without *grit*. You need passion and grit (perseverance) to stay focused year after year to gain the skills and knowledge that take you to the top. Therefore, grit seems to play a more important role than talent. This view is reflected in the theory of the *growth mindset*: the belief that people's most basic abilities can be developed through dedication and hard work.

Accomplishment

The previous chapter described how happiness is different for each person, but research shows that one factor virtually guarantees its boost: *working toward a goal*. Lyubomirsky (2008) found that people who strive for something personally significant are far happier than those who do not have strong dreams or aspirations. Pursuing a goal provides our lives with six benefits:

1. Greater feelings of purpose and control
2. Increased self-esteem and confidence
3. Greater structure and meaning
4. Sharper planning and prioritizing skills
5. Increased ability to cope with problems
6. Opportunities to engage with others

Lyubomirski, King, and Diener (2005) studied the relationship between happiness and success in different fields, such as marriage, friendship, income, work performance, and health. They found not only that success makes people happier, but also that it works the other way around: Positive emotions enhance success. Happiness is related to and precedes many successful outcomes. It also turns out that positive affect underlies many characteristics, resources, and successes related to happiness.

Wiseman (2009), using the data from 5,000 respondents, found that successful people perform the following five things:

1. They have a goal and name specific subgoals that they realize step by step.
2. They inform friends, family, and colleagues about their goals. The advantage of this is that others can help when there are obstacles on the way to the goal. Informing others about your goals also has the advantage that it generates more determination.
3. They imagine what the positive consequences are of achieving their goals.

4. They reward themselves when they have reached a subgoal and plan beforehand how they will reward themselves.
5. They record their progress as concretely as possible in a diary or on a computer, or they graph their improvements.

APPLICATION 170. PERFORM FIVE THINGS FOR (MORE) SUCCESS

Invite clients to act on Wiseman's findings (2009) and perform the following five things for (more) success:

1. Find a goal and name specific subgoals.
2. Inform friends, family, and colleagues about their goals.
3. Imagine the positive consequences of achieving their goals.
4. Reward themselves when they have reached a subgoal.
5. Record their progress as concretely as possible.

APPLICATION 171. FIND POSITIVE DIFFERENCES

Invite clients to imagine that they are a fly on the wall at home, at work, or at school and ask themselves the following two questions:

1. What does the fly on the wall see you and the people around you doing when there is a problem or a conflict? What is everyone doing, how are they looking, and how are they reacting to each other?
2. What does the fly on the wall see you and the people around you

doing differently when the problem or conflict is gone or is less of a problem? How does the fly notice that things are better? What is everyone doing, how are they looking, and how are they reacting to each other now?

Invite clients to compare these two pictures and find as many positive differences as possible. How will the fly on the wall know which is the preferred picture? And how can they (and others) ensure that the preferred picture becomes reality?

A POSITIVE DIFFERENCE

A boy was picking something up and throwing it into the ocean. A man approached him and asked, "What are you doing?" The boy replied, "I am saving the starfish that have been stranded on the beach. The tide is going out, and if I don't throw them back, they will die." The man noticed that there were miles and miles of beach and thousands of starfish. He looked at the beach again and then at the boy and said, "Well, you won't make much of a difference, will you?"

The little boy picked up another starfish and threw it into the sea. Then, looking up, he smiled and said, "I made a difference for that one!"

APPLICATION 172. IDENTIFY SUCCESS, TALENT, AND AMBITION

Invite individual clients to tell you about their successes, talents, and ambitions. Or invite a group or a team (this can be done as an introduction exercise) to interview each other in pairs for three minutes about their success, talent, and ambition. Then ask each group member to introduce their partner to the group in one minute on the basis of what they just heard about that person's success, talent, and ambition. In this way, people also exercise their listening skills.

APPLICATION 173. MAKE A BEST SELF-PORTRAIT

Sometimes people only hear positive things about themselves when they change jobs and their boss speaks highly of them and how they will be dearly missed. Sometimes positive things are mentioned solely at someone's funeral. But it does not have to be this way!

Invite clients to ask ten to twenty people in their life (family, friends, colleagues) to give them three written stories that describe how the client made a positive contribution in some way. Ask them to collect all the stories and bring them together, looking for common themes, surprises, and insights. Then ask them to synthesize all the different contributions into a *best self-portrait*, summarizing their findings or creating a project based on the synthesis and sharing the results with important people in their life. People often combine this exercise with their VIA survey results to get a clear picture of their character strengths in action as well as to see how closely the strengths they perceive they have line up with the strengths others perceive them to have.

Note that twenty people may sound like a daunting number, but think of the impact this might have. Clients will be having meaningful conversations with twenty people in their life; they will be soliciting positive, engaging comments from these people; they will probably be connecting with people across numerous domains of their life—personal, social, work, and spiritual. Consider how transformative this can be for them, for the others, and for their relationships.

APPLICATION 174. FIND PREVIOUS SUCCESSES

Invite clients to search for and find previous successes in their life and in dealing with difficult situations. Invite them to be curious and ask themselves the following *competence questions*: "How did I succeed?" "What exactly did I do to make that happen?" "How did I come up with that good idea?" "What talents, strengths, and resources did I use?" Also invite them to ask themselves, "What could I apply in my current situation?"

APPLICATION 175. MAKE A SUCCESS BOX

A variation of the *compliment box* (see Application 130) is the *success box*. First, the group members (a team, therapy group, or family) make or buy a beautiful box. All group members are invited to anonymously submit three separate notes with solutions that have helped them successfully face or solve problems. Examples of solutions are talking to a friend, taking long walks, or keeping a positive diary. When all notes have been placed in the box, they are removed and placed on a table. All group members can pick up one or two of these notes with solutions that are new to them (or that they want to try again) and try them out in a behavioral experiment. The next time the group comes together, they share whether this has been helpful. In this way, the expertise of the whole group is used optimally.

APPLICATION 176. PASS ON COMPETENCIES

Invite group or team members to pair up to explore each other's competence. This exercise requires groups of four who break into two pairs. The steps are as follows:

1. Everyone thinks back to a (recent) success in life or work.
2. One member of the pair interviews his or her colleague to find out what worked. What exactly did this colleague do to help their client(s) be successful? The colleague then interviews the other person to find out what worked for him or her (2 x 7 minutes).
3. The four people then come together; each person in the pair shares their colleague's success factors with two other colleagues (10 minutes).

With this exercise, people hear four success stories in quick succession: their own story, the story of the colleague they interviewed, and the stories of two other colleagues. In addition, this application allows for some physical activity as people mingle with their colleagues to recount their partner's success factors.

APPLICATION 177. MAKE A CERTIFICATE OF COMPETENCE

Invite clients to make their own Certificate of Competence (www.john-wheeler.co.uk). This certificate is a (self)-coaching tool for optimizing professional practice using seven questions:

1. When I do my work, I take my inspiration from the following people: . . .
2. These people have taught me that when I do my work, it is most important to remember the following: . . .
3. These are the people who encourage me to do the work I do: . . .
4. They encouraged me to do this work because they noticed the following about me: . . .
5. When I do my work, the people I deal with are likely to appreciate that I have the following qualities and abilities: . . .
6. These are the people in my support network who know I have these qualities and abilities: . . .
7. If I am under pressure at work and can only remember one quality or ability, it should be this: . . .

Focus on Success

To what extent should you focus on problems and mistakes instead of on accomplishments and successes? How much attention should you pay to what is wrong? Famous management consultant Drucker (Cooperrider & Whitney, 2005, p. 2) was clear about this. He stated that there is a tipping point in focusing on strengths: "The great task of leadership is to create an alignment of strengths in ways that make a system's weaknesses irrelevant." Appreciative inquiry (see Chapter 1) and solution-focused interviewing also focus primarily on successes.

Bannink (2010c) described the same approach when it comes to *chance management* and *risk management* in organizations. In many organizations, most attention is paid to risks and hazards and the ways in which these can be prevented or limited. As a result, there is often little focus on chances and opportunities. In a solution-focused organization, exactly the opposite takes place: The focus is predominantly—80 percent—on possibilities and opportunities and only 20 percent on risks and hazards. In this way, risk managers also become *chance managers.*

10 MILLION DOLLARS LOST

In the 1960s, an executive at IBM made a decision that ended up losing the company 10 million dollars. The CEO of IBM, Tom Watson, summoned the offending executive to his office at corporate headquarters. A journalist described what happened next: As the executive cowered, Watson asked, "Do you know why I've asked you here?" The man replied, "I assume I'm here so you can fire me." Watson looked surprised. "Fire you? Of course not. I just spent 10 million dollars educating you" (Heath & Heath, 2010).

APPLICATION 178. TURN AROUND THE 80-20 DEFICIT RULE

As stated previously, the 80-20 deficit rule ensures that in our society the focus is predominantly on problems and errors, but that rule can be reversed. Invite clients to consider what ratio they apply in their work and/or personal life. Also ask them to check whether they are satisfied with it and whether it permits them to function optimally and decide whether they want to change this rule and pay more attention to what is going right instead of wrong.

WINNIE-THE-POOH ON SUCCESS

Different people define success in different ways. But more and more, it has become synonymous with money and status. Real success, however, is less about results or a bottom line and more about the process of achieving goals and dreams.

It is not only humans who think that building success is important; some fictitious animals consider it to be "the most important subject of all." In Winnie-the-Pooh on Success (Allen & Allen, 1997, p. 17), the Wise Stranger tells the animals how they can become successful. He writes the following acronym on a sheet of paper and shows it to his friends:

Select a Dream

Use your dreams to set a Goal

Create a Plan

Consider Resources

Enhance Skills and Abilities

Spend time Wisely

Start! Get Organized and Go

APPLICATION 179. SAVOR SUCCESSFUL MEMORIES

Invite clients to recall some successful events in their lives. Invite them to remember where they were, who was there with them, and what they were thinking, doing, and feeling. After they recall the event, ask them to take a few minutes to simply savor the positive memories and pleasant feelings this experience brings forth in them.

APPLICATION 180. START A POSITIVE CONVERSATION AT WORK

Invite clients to start a positive conversation with colleagues about their work. Possible topics are as follows:

- A satisfying moment at work
- Recent progress in something important to them
- A conversation they were pleased about
- Something they have tried recently and that has been successful

APPLICATION 181. WRITE HOW YOU ARE DOING IN TEN YEARS

King (2001) suggested writing about how you will be doing in ten years' time when everything in your life has gone well—when things are going well at work, you are successful, and in other areas of your life everything is as good as can be. Invite clients to do the same. When they have filled in all the details, ask them to reread what they wrote and to extract a goal or mission on which they can work every day. Clients may also make a five- or even ten-year plan to ensure that their mission will succeed (see Application 76).

APPLICATION 182. CELEBRATE SUCCESS

Solution-focused professionals always start with the end in mind—for example, by asking clients at the start of the contact how they will celebrate when they have achieved their goal. Children especially (and their parents) find this a nice way to start the conversation. They are also asked whom they will invite to the party, what refreshments they are going to serve, and whom they are going to thank for their help in achieving this goal. Application 81 is a nice variation for teams.

APPLICATION 183. CREATE A SUCCESS CERTIFICATE

At the end of a trauma treatment, for example, create a signed *posttraumatic success certificate* for clients (Bannink, 2014b) on which the client's achieved goal and the steps taken by the client to get there are written.

Positive Supervision

It is often said, "One learns best from one's mistakes." However, research shows that one probably learns more from one's successes (Histed, Pasupathy, & Miller, 2009). Despite this, in supervision the main concern is what does not work and how to rectify it. Also, in most supervision, the 80-20 deficit-rule is still being used.

Positive supervision focuses on what actually works instead of on problems and on supervisees' strengths rather than on their deficits. The task of supervisors using this approach—unlike traditional problem solving—is to create solutions with their supervisees and to teach them to apply the same approach when working with their own clients. Positive supervision, based on positive psychology and solution-focused interviewing, reinforces the competence and skills of the supervisees. It is short, positive, hopeful, and cost-effective, with less burnout for supervisors. This innovative approach to individual, group, and peer supervision is suitable for use in any environment (clinical, corporate, educational, health, governmental, community).

Bannink's model is based on four pillars: (1) goal formulation, (2) finding competence, (3) working on progress, and (4) reflection. Positive supervision is appropriate for all supervisors who together with their supervisees or trainees want to focus on successes and competence instead of on failures and shortcomings. As one supervisee remarked:

> In traditional supervision I learned from the "sharp minds" of
> my supervisors; in positive supervision I learned to use my own

"sharp mind." This helps me to become more independent and more effective in creating and supporting change. (Bannink, 2015a)

APPLICATION 184. REPORT SPARKLING MOMENTS

Invite clients to report a recent sparkling moment in their life (or work):

- Think about one of the sparkling moments in the past few weeks—a moment when they really felt at their best.
- What was it that made the moment sparkle for them?
- What are they most satisfied with when they think back to that moment?
- What would others (important people or colleagues) have thought about them if they had seen that moment?
- When these qualities play an even bigger role in their life or work, who will be the first to notice this? How will they notice?
- What small step might they take to increase the prospect of (even) more sparkling moments?

FOCUS ON STRENGTHS IN SUPERVISION

In supervision with two people, the supervisor creates a positive start. She asks what both supervisees like about their work and what they are good at. One of the supervisees mentions that she herself is good at collaborating with her clients, is able to react swiftly if necessary, is empathetic, and is doing her utmost to be helpful. The other supervisee mentions that she herself is a good listener, is creative in finding solutions together with her clients, and is patient and persistent.

Then the supervisor asks what both see as the strengths of each other; after all, they work together and know each other. The first supervisee mentions as strengths of the other supervisee that she is firm and empathetic and can easily make contact with clients and colleagues. The other supervisee mentions as strengths of the first supervisee that she is calm, is a good listener, and is patient and honest.

The nice thing about the last question is that colleagues often come up with other things than what the supervisees would come up with themselves. It is often a surprise to hear what strengths other people see in you.

APPLICATION 185. COLLECT PROOF OF COMPETENCE

Ask supervisees what they see as the best way for you as their supervisor to collect proof of their competence. What should you, as their supervisor, pay attention to? What, according to them, can you do to achieve this? How would they like to receive your feedback?

APPLICATION 186. LISTEN WITH STRENGTH EARS

This application is about using your ears to hear only about the strengths a person has and nothing else. You can perform this exercise in group or peer supervision. First, invite one of the supervisees to tell the others about a recent successful or pleasant event, something he is proud of or happy about. The others are asked to respond by giving as many compliments as possible. This includes direct compliments, competence questions, and positive statements about the personality of the supervisee. The supervisee is then asked what compliments had the strongest impact on him.

Then another person (or the same person) is invited to tell about a recent nasty event, something about which he is ashamed, angry, or sad. The others are asked again to come up with as many compliments as possible. Then the person is asked what compliments made the strongest impression on him.

This is an exercise to notice how much harder it sometimes is to (continuously) give compliments to people who tell something negative. Ask supervisees for their thoughts about which person needs the compliments the most.

APPLICATION 187. MAXIMIZE SUCCESS

You can do this in an abbreviated form in which all supervisees concisely describe a recent success. In the longer version, one or a few successes are investigated (roughly twenty minutes are allotted to each case). The five steps are as follows:

1. All supervisees briefly mention a success. A few successes are chosen for further discussion, depending on how much time is available.
2. For each successful case, the supervisees ask each other questions, and

together they examine what the success entails exactly, what helpful interventions have been applied, and what the success signifies for the supervisee and the client.

3. The supervisees take turns complimenting the supervisee who presented the case on what he or she did well and on other things about the presenter that they respect and value.
4. Each supervisee briefly relates what he or she has learned from discussing the successful case and how he or she may put that knowledge to use.
5. All supervisees indicate what they considered useful and beneficial about the session and which of those things they might implement. Then the session is concluded or the next case is presented.

APPLICATION 188. DISCUSS THE MOST CHALLENGING CASE

With this application, the most difficult case—supervisees *most challenging case*—is presented and a limited amount of time is allotted to each case (five minutes maximum). This exercise can be done in pairs or in a group, with everyone taking a turn.

The goal is to go through a large number of cases in a short amount of time. This method takes up little time and calls for a lot of input. The focus is on how the supervisees can move up one point on the scale. Background information about the case is unnecessary; what matters is what the supervisees presenting the case are able or willing to do to move one point higher on the scale.

With challenging cases, there is almost always an impasse or a negative alliance with the clients. The objective is for the supervisees to recognize small improvements. Ask the supervisee, "Supposing the next session ends one point higher on the scale than the last one, what will you have done differently?" "What else will you have done differently?" "And what else?" Note that this question is not about what clients should have done differently.

If the presenter of the case also wants input from the other supervisees, they are invited to present their ideas.

APPLICATION 189. INTERVIEW ABOUT SUCCESS

Interview supervisees or colleagues about their successes using the following questions:

- Ask supervisees to choose a situation at work when they were successful.
- Explore in detail how they did it: how, what, when, where, with whom.
- What else was important?
- Which of their competencies and strengths were helpful?
- What would their client say they did that was helpful?
- On a scale from 10 to 0, how confident are they that this will happen again?
- What should they focus on to increase the chances that it will happen again?

APPLICATION 190. FEEL PROUD

You might say that pride is the opposite of guilt—you are "guilty" of having done something good instead of something bad (see Application 62). Pride is the good feeling you get when you have made a good report or when you notice your customers are satisfied. Pride is socially important too, because you usually like to share with others what you are proud of. You assume that they will also appreciate your success. Research shows that people who feel proud continue to work on a difficult task longer than people who do not feel proud (Williams & DeSteno, 2008). However, pride is sometimes viewed with mixed feelings; in some cultures, pride is not valued highly. But invite clients to put their modesty aside for a while and find out what they are proud of.

PROUD

Two years after giving a solution-focused training course for lawyers, I met one of the participants at a congress. He told me the following story. On his way home after the last training day, he had been thinking about how he could apply what he had learned at home. He decided to ask his three young children, before putting them to bed, what they had been proud of that day. He told me that this had become a daily ritual, in which his children also asked him what he had done that he had been proud of. If he forgot to ask his children, they would remind him and say, "Daddy, we haven't talked about what we are proud of yet."

He told me that this ritual colored his day as well: What could he tell his children that night? If he had done nothing so far that day that he was proud of, he still had the opportunity to do something about it.

APPLICATION 191. ASK WHAT THEY TAKE HOME

A nice question at the end of a training course or team meeting, coaching, supervision or other conversation is, "What do you take home from this meeting?" Invite the participants to describe five things or ideas that they can put to use that will tell them that the meeting has been worth their time, effort, energy, and money. This is a form of *capitalization* (see Application 101).

APPLICATION 192. VIEW THE PROBLEM FROM A DIFFERENT PERSPECTIVE

It is often useful and fun to view a problem and the possible solutions from a different perspective—not from the perspective of the therapist, supervisor, coach, or client, but from the perspective of a different job. Invite supervisees (or clients) to first choose another job (e.g., the job they wanted to have as a child). One can also work with cards, on which a number of professions are already written. Once the new job is selected, they are invited to look first at the problem and then at solutions from the viewpoint of their new job. The creativity and new perspectives that this application produces is often surprising.

Passion and Grit

We all know success is not possible without passion and grit (perseverance). Perseverance is one of the four character strengths belonging to the virtue of courage (see Table 1.1). Duckworth and Gross (2014) defined grit as "a passion for and perseverance in achieving long-term goals."

You need *passion* to stay focused year after year to gain the skills and knowledge that will take you to the top. The concept of passion is one we regularly use to describe our interests, and yet there is no broad theory that can explain the development and consequences of passion for activities across people's lives.

Vallerand (2015) presented the first such theory, providing a presentation of the dualistic model of passion and the empirical evidence that supports it. He conceived of two types of passion: *harmonious passion*, which remains under the person's control, and *obsessive passion*, which controls the person. While the first typically leads to adaptive behaviors, the obsessive form of passion leads to less adaptive and, at times, maladaptive behaviors. The effects of these two types of passion are numerous on a number of psychological phenomena, such as cognition, emotions, performance, relationships, aggression, and violence.

Because *grit* is always about long-term goals, there will be setbacks and stagnation is almost inevitable, but gritty people go on until they succeed. Even if they fall, they always get up again. Think of Edison, who tried a thousand times before he invented the lightbulb. He is supposed to have said that genius is 1 percent inspiration and 99 percent perspiration.

Persistent people often are obsessed by an idea and make it their life's work. Grit is about running a marathon, not about running a sprint. Grit is about stamina, not about intensity.

However, grit is not the same as self-control. You can have a lot of self-control but no passion, so you may go from one career to another without really achieving anything. Or you may be very persistent in your work but have insufficient self-control to resist temptations, such as eating or chatting during work. Grit is not the same as talent either. Talent is important because talented people learn quickly. However, grit appears to be a better predictor of success than is talent as measured by an IQ test or an admission test for a particular field of education. In addition, not everyone has the same amount of talent, so it's better that people focus on something over which they do have influence: grit. Here a *growth mindset* (see below) plays a major role. Grit has to do with the (admittedly questionable, but still usable) idea that 10,000 hours of *deliberate practice* (deliberate exercise, in which not only the quantity but also the quality of the exercise is important) are needed to reach excellence (Gladwell, 2008).

APPLICATION 193. PERSEVERE

In the long term, accomplishment has more to do with becoming good at something than being good at something, provided there is a fairly basic level of ability to begin with. Here are some tips to increase clients' chances of success in the long term:

- Work on realistic goals.
- Know what to expect. If you want to reach the top, know that it takes time, effort, and perseverance, and that there may be setbacks. Work

especially on your strengths and make sure that you improve weaknesses. That's not always fun.

- Also continue on bad days. Promise yourself to continue for, for example, six months or two years. If you then want to stop, that's okay, but not earlier.

- Ask friends to be there for you if your perseverance is low and help you to continue until the deadline is reached.

- Use a coach. Deliberate practice is sometimes hard and feedback is important. Professional support can be very effective.

- Do not let obstacles hold you back. Use "if-then" implementations (see Application 66).

- Focus on getting a little bit better each day and look at your achievements with a growth mindset. If you practice outside your comfort zone, failures do not mean that you are not good at something; on the contrary, they are signs that you are improving!

APPLICATION 194. DO SOMETHING ELSE

Einstein stated that insanity is doing the same thing over and over again, expecting different results. So if something is not working and there is no progress, stop and do something else. In those cases, persevering is not very useful.

Invite clients to consider what they might do differently and find out what difference this makes. Others such as therapists, coaches, and managers do not have to give suggestions or advice. The two basic solution-focused principles apply: If something works (better), do more or it; if something is not working, do something else.

APPLICATION 195. PRACTICE FOR THE GUINNESS WORLD RECORDS

Are you already mentioned in the *Guinness World Records*? Invite clients to think about how and when they would like to be included in the *Guinness World Records*. Even unrealistic goals are allowed when dreaming about accomplishments. Clients may also discuss this with their family or colleagues. People will probably never reach the *Guinness World Records* if they have no grit. This question is sometimes asked during job interviews, where candidates who do not have an answer will probably not get the job.

Growth Mindset

A *mindset*, according to Dweck (2006), is a self-perception or *self-theory* that people hold about themselves. Believing that you are either "intelligent" or "unintelligent" is a simple example of a mindset. People may also have a mindset related to their personal or professional lives—for example, "I'm a good teacher" or "I'm a bad parent." People can be aware or unaware of their mindsets, but they can have profound effect on learning achievement, skill acquisition, personal relationships, professional success, and many other dimensions of life.

The growth mindset is the belief that qualities can change and that we can develop our intelligence and abilities. The opposite of having a growth mindset is having a fixed mindset, which is the belief that intelligence and abilities cannot be developed. The reason that this definition of growth mindset is important is that research shows that this belief leads people to take on challenges, work harder and more effectively, and persevere in the face of adversity, all of which makes people more successful learners (see Table 6.1).

Dweck (2006) found that students with a fixed mindset have stronger and more depressive complaints than students with a growth mindset. Students with a fixed mindset stagnated when encountering failures, and the more depressed they became, the more they gave up, making no further attempts to solve their problems. Students with a growth mindset who suffered from depressive complaints displayed different behaviors. The more depressed they reported themselves as being, the more action they undertook to solve their problems, the harder they worked, and the more active they became in structuring their lives. In the great YouTube film "The Power of Yet," the characters of Sesame Street explain the growth mindset (see https://www.youtube.com/watch?v=XLeUvZvuvAs).

Dweck also mentioned some misconceptions about the growth mindset. A growth mindset is not just about effort. Perhaps the most common misconception is simply equating the growth mindset with effort. Although effort is key for achievement, it's not the only thing. People need to try new strategies and seek input from others when they are stuck. They need this repertoire of approaches—not just sheer effort—to learn and improve. Furthermore, a growth mindset is not the same as being open-minded and positive. It is not only about giving compliments and rewarding effort, either.

And finally, having a growth mindset is no guarantee that only good things will happen in your life.

There is discussion about the compatibility of the concepts of talent and strengths, and the growth mindset. Some people claim that talents and strengths fit very well within the theory of the growth mindset, because talents and strengths can be developed. Others argue that using concepts such as talents and strengths makes it more difficult to focus on issues such as sharing information, seeking feedback, admitting mistakes, and working together and therefore belongs to a fixed mindset.

Bostwick (2015) found that students who believe that their intelligence is able to grow over time (growth mindset) perform better on measures of academic success than students who believe that intelligence is a fixed trait that cannot be changed. She tested the effectiveness of a growth mindset intervention in an applied higher education setting. Students enrolled in an introductory psychology course ($N = 278$) were randomly assigned to receive one of three letters after the completion of their first midterm exam. The messages in the letters were centered on either promoting a growth mindset, promoting a fixed mindset, or just thanking students for their class attendance and participation. Additionally, a manipulation check was administered nine weeks post-intervention to see if students read their letter and remembered its take-home message. At the end of the term, between-group differences on measures of post-intervention academic success were assessed. Students in the malleable mindset condition outperformed students in the fixed mindset condition on two measures of post-intervention academic success. This effect was stronger for those students who passed the manipulation check at the end of the term. Therefore, the intervention design was an effective way to promote a growth mindset in students and increase academic success in higher education.

TABLE 6.2
Differences Between A Fixed and A Growth Mindset.

Fixed Mindset	Growth Mindset
Success is winning	Success is making progress
Avoids challenges	Embraces challenges
Failure is indication of lack of talent	Failure is indication of learning
Sees effort as fruitless	Sees effort as path to mastery
Gives up easily due to obstacles	Persists despite obstacles
Ignores feedback, or sees feedback as indication of lack of talent	Learns from feedback
Threatened by others' success, which shows they have more talent	Inspired by others' success, which shows they have had more practice

APPLICATION 196. BUILD A GROWTH MINDSET

Here are some thoughts and questions for building a growth mindset. Invite clients to consider the following statements and questions and see how they may already use a growth mindset or may change their fixed mindset:

- If you take on challenges, making mistakes is inevitable.
- This is a difficult subject, but that makes it fun.
- I learned a lot from that difficult period.
- No one is too old to learn.
- Will you give me feedback?
- You may learn from the successes of others.
- What is going well and does not need to change?
- What works, if only a little bit?
- How did you succeed?
- What can you do (even) better next time?
- How can I use this to my own advantage?
- How can we learn from each other?

APPLICATION 197. ENCOURAGE A GROWTH MINDSET

As a manager, trainer, therapist, or coach (or teacher or parent) pay compliments on what a person (or child) *does* and not about who someone *is*. Do not say to a tennis player, "You have such a beautiful backhand; you must have a lot of talent" but rather "You have such a beautiful backhand; how did you learn that?" Compliments that focus on the process or a particular behavior encourage a growth mindset, whereas compliments that focus on the person stimulate a fixed mindset.

APPLICATION 198. OPT FOR BETTER

With a growth mindset, people want to become better in certain areas of their life (see Table 6.2). Invite clients to tell you what is going better instead of what is going well. After all, if better is possible, then often good is not good enough. With this solution-focused question, clients are invited to talk about their progress instead of possible stagnation.

APPLICATION 199. REQUEST FEEDBACK

Requesting feedback is a valuable addition to a professional's self-reflection, which can be obstructed by blind spots and avoidance tendencies. Requesting feedback from clients and supervisees is a basic social skill that may be helpful in adjusting dysfunctional interactions (Bannink & Den Haan, 2016). Also, in this way, the competence of the professional comes to the fore, and this is how they may become (even) better at their job. Furthermore, feedback may provide solutions in the case of disagreements and conflicts, and, last but not least, feedback contributes to mutual equality.

APPLICATION 200. THINK OF SOLUTIONS

As a manager, trainer, therapist, coach, or supervisor (or teacher or parent), invite employees, clients, or supervisees (or children) to come up with at least two solutions themselves when presenting a problem, before you add anything—if that is even still necessary. In this way, you encourage them to pause and reflect and to become better at what they are doing instead of solely looking to you for solutions.

APPLICATION 201. OBSERVE YOUR IDOL

Who was your idol when you were young? Invite clients to start observing the development of their idol (in sports, music, etc). This allows them to stimulate a growth mindset, because they will probably find out that talent does not come naturally but is purposefully developed and that grit has played a major role in their idol's attempts at achieving success.

WELL DONE

A supervisor in a company explains what he is doing differently now when his employees submit an incomplete report. "I make sure to start commenting on what the employee has done well, and only then do I ask what further information he needs to add to improve the report even more." This supervisor now sends out a different message about the competencies and capabilities of his employees to make a valuable contribution to the organization than does the traditional method of supervision, which focuses on mistakes or failures and how to avoid or repair them (Bannink, 2015a).

7

Further Applications

No bird soars too high if he soars with his own wings.

—WILLIAM BLAKE

The science of PP is relatively new. The first results of research and the first applications date back to the early years of this century. In recent years, more and more questionnaires have been developed with a focus on strengths instead of on shortcomings. Some of these questionnaires are described in this chapter. A second area in which PP is applied is in the use of cards and (online) games in psychotherapy, coaching, and training.

Online applications of PP are a third promising field. Research shows no difference in effectiveness between online interventions and interventions delivered by a therapist. It therefore makes sense to provide PP interventions (PPIs) via smartphones and other Internet possibilities.

E-health modules—online treatment programs—combine online psychotherapy with personal sessions with a therapist (*blended care*). In this way, clients can receive treatment from their homes. In addition, there are many self-help courses on the Internet based on PP. Also, *m-Health* (treatment programs available on smartphones and tablets) has been introduced in healthcare. Applications (apps) are being developed in the field of PP, and there is preliminary evidence that these applications enhance people's mood and happiness. In this chapter, these promising developments are examined further.

Questionnaires

Most instruments for measurement in mental health focus on pathology. For example, there are many questionnaires for measuring anxiety and depression. However, nowadays, questionnaires that combine questions about complaints and well-being are also available. The development of instruments with which to measure positive mental health is important, but there is still little research on standardized instruments to measure the strengths of clients. Also, the validity of those instruments is still seldom substantiated in clinical populations.

Research shows that a focus on strengths helps prevent the development of psychopathology and protects against relapse (Fredrickson, 2001). It was also found that a focus on strengths contributes to a positive alliance with clients and increases their willingness to accept therapeutic interventions (Flückiger, Caspar, Grosse Holtforth, & Willutzki, 2009). Graybeal (2001) found that diagnostics directed to strengths have a therapeutic value of their own.

In Chapter 1, some questionnaires were discussed: the VIA questionnaire (www.viacharacter.org), the StrengthsFinder (www.strengthsfinder. com), and the R2 Strengths Profiler (formerly Realise2; www.capp.co/ R2StrengthsProfiler). Lamers, Smit, and Hutschemaekers (2013) distinguished between questionnaires to measure emotional well-being (including the PANAS: Positive and Negative Affect Schedule and SWLS: Satisfaction With Life Scale), questionnaires to measure psychological well-being (Psychological Well-Being Scale and Basic Need Satisfaction Scale), and questionnaires to measure social well-being (Social Well-Being Scale). These three components of well-being were described in Chapter 1.

The authors described questionnaires measuring multiple components of positive mental health, such as the Control Autonomy Self-Realization and Pleasure Scale (CASP), the Warwick-Edinburgh Mental Well-Being Scale (WEMWBS), the Flourishing Scale, and the Mental Health Continuum–Short Form (MHC SF). Their conclusion is threefold. First, there is still much that is indistinct about the relationship between the three components of well-being. Second, the authors are aware that their choice to limit their focus to indicators of positive mental health and not include process variables is debatable. Third, in their findings, they emphasize the importance of using questionnaires to measure positive mental health in combination with questionnaires to measure psychopathology, since both are separate and distinct indicators of mental health.

Another promising questionnaire is the *Strengths Q-sort Self-Assessment Scale* (SQSS; Bellier-Teichmann & Pomini, 2015). The authors wanted to develop a simple and quick test of strengths as identified in the PP literature that shows a profile of strengths useful for psychotherapy. The test measures thirty strengths, divided into three groups: personal characteristics, hobbies and environment, and social strengths. The test consists of thirty cards that are shown to the client. Each card shows the name of a particular strength along with a picture of it. There are three steps involved in the exercise, and each addresses a different dimension:

1. The presence and absence of strengths
2. The extent to which strengths contribute to personal well-being
3. The desire to develop new strengths

A semistructured interview with the client follows, in which their strengths are further discussed. The questionnaire, which was administered to twenty-one psychiatric patients with various DSM-5 classifications, appeared to be easy to fill out and was appreciated by clients.

Many questionnaires have been developed these days, including ones to measure positive emotions, hope, commitment, compassion, meaning, gratitude, and satisfaction.

Examples are the Positive and Negative Affect Schedule (PANAS), the Gratitude Questionnaire (GQ-6), the Hope Scale (HS), the Inspiration Scale (IS), the Meaning in Life Questionnaire (MLQ), the Self-Compassion Scale (SCS), the Purpose in Life Test (PIL), the Life Purpose Questionnaire (LPQ), the Seeking of Noetic Goals test (SONG), the Meaning in Suffering Test (MIST), the Life Attitude Profile Revised (LAP-R), the Mindful Attention Awareness Scale (MAAS), the Quality of Life Inventory (QOLI), and the Personal Growth Initiative Scale (PGIS).

Cards and (Online) Games

The use of cards in the SQSS was described above. There are also cards depicting strengths that are used for coaching or training purposes, individually or in a group. The fifty *Strengths Cards* by Boniwell (www.positran.fr) each contain a picture together with the name of the strength on one side, and the other side contains questions to identify the strength, a description of the strength, and some suggestions as to how this strength may be activated and developed (stretched). For example, the card containing the strength *empathy* is described below.

Question: Does this sound like you? 1. You are always the first person in any group to realise that another group member is upset. 2. You cry while watching a touching movie. 3. You can be equally excited about the success of others as about your own. *Description:* If this sounds like you, you might have the strength of Empathy. That means you have the experience of understanding another person from their perspective. You can place yourself in their shoes and feel what they are feeling. You are always able to see things from another's point of view. You are able to fully share the happiness and frustration of others. *Activate*: 1. Observe the behavior of a stranger and try to understand what's going on. 2. While speaking with people try to grasp what they are really saying, not just with words but also with their faces and bodies. *Stretch*: 1. Invite a homeless person to a restaurant and listen to their life story. 2. Take up a counselling course to apply your strength professionally.

Build & Share is a group facilitation method, using LEGO® play, that builds on theory, research, and application within PP and narrative practices. When applied in groups, the method helps participants to gain a deeper, more meaningful understanding of topics, especially those related to motivation, resilience, and engagement. Build & Share provides an engaging and memorable approach to shared understanding and self-exploration in areas related to well-being and optimal functioning. Build & Share deepens the reflection process and supports effective dialogue for everyone in the group. This is done by posing reflective questions and allowing participants to build their answer in LEGO® materials and respond by using metaphors and narratives they have created themselves rather than answering questions in a traditional way.

Super Better is an interactive online game, based on PP research findings, for helping participants to work on resilience after an illness or adversity and attain certain health goals. Recovery is seen as a game; players set goals, and there are several quests in which they have to fight virtual enemies to achieve their goals. The power of positive emotions and social connection is used; family or friends and buddies may be used as supporters. Players can get to higher levels, gaining rewards, until they have reached their goal. Two other online games, *Uplifted* and *e-Positive Spin*, are described below.

E-health

E-health means *electronic health*, or health care provided by the Internet. Ritterband and colleagues (2003, p. 527) defined online interventions as:

> interventions typically focused on behavioral issues, with the goal of instituting behavior change and subsequent symptom improvement. They are usually self-paced, interactive and tailored to the user, and they make use of the multimedia format offered by the Internet.

Most online interventions include psychoeducation and information, self-testing of health and well-being with automatic feedback, and/or a self-help course or treatment. Online self-help programs may include advice for a positive attitude to life and discuss items such as positive thinking, self-compassion, happiness, joy, and wisdom. Bolier (2015) stated that although it is clear that more intensive and face-to-face interventions generate larger effects, the effects of short-term self-help interventions are small but significant. From a public health perspective, self-help interventions can serve as cost-effective mental health promotion tools to reach large target groups that may not otherwise be reached.

New technologies to improve consumers' health, without the intervention of professionals, are being rapidly provided. Not all online interventions, however, have the goal to help others; sometimes they are also—or even solely—commercial. It is important that the quality of these applications be better monitored. A methodology for the scientific evaluation of these technologies should be developed, as should a quality label for medical applications.

Seligman and colleagues (2005) were the first to research the effectiveness of online positive psychology interventions (OPPIs). They found the strongest effects in the applications "List three blessings" (see Application 30) and "Use character strengths in a new way" (see Application 140). The positive effects on well-being and depression were still significant after six months. In later studies, these results were only partially replicated; only the positive effect on well-being remained.

Mitchell, Vella-Broderick, and Klein provided an overview of OPPIs in 2010. They found ambiguous results: In three of the five studies, a significant increase in well-being and reduction in symptoms was found, but two other studies showed no, or even negative, results.

Bolier (2015) conducted a meta-analysis of thirty-nine PPI studies and discovered that the findings concerning effectiveness were also true for OPPIs. She found that the results of the literature review were positive; however, the quality of the research on the effectiveness of these programs was not high. For example, the randomization procedure was unclear in many studies. Also, most studies conducted completers-only analysis as opposed to intention-to-treat analysis, and the number of studies in some subgroups was small. More high-quality randomized controlled trials are needed to enable more robust conclusions about the effects of PPIs.

Bolier (2015) also examined *Psyfit*, an OPPI to help participants train for mental fitness, analogous to training for physical fitness. Participants received suggestions to improve their mental fitness and confront daily hassles based on six principles, such as giving direction to one's life, investing in positive relations, and living in the here-and-now. The intervention was effective in increasing well-being and vitality in the short term and in reducing anxiety and depression in the short and longer term. There were indications that people with higher education and people over forty-five years of age benefited more from the intervention. The cost-effectiveness of the intervention was not clear.

The same intervention was studied in a number of complaints-focused situations. Nurses and paramedics working in a hospital received an online questionnaire with feedback on the results of a range of online interventions, including Psyfit. The positive mental health of the participants improved significantly when followed up at three and six months. However, there were no positive effects on work performance and psychological problems. The compliance was very low (only 5 percent of the participants used an intervention to some extent).

Bolier concluded that (O)PPIs can be effective in promoting well-being and reducing psychological symptoms. This is important not only for the large-scale promotion of mental health in the population but also in the promotion of physical health and recovery after, for example, heart disease. To ensure the impact of OPPIs, the compliance (adherence) rate of the interventions should be enhanced and OPPIs should be embedded in health care systems. The potential is huge; not only can mental health services apply them, but they will also enable the somatic health services to pay more attention to the well-being and resilience of patients.

Four OPPIs deserve further attention because they explicitly mention research or theory: Uplifted, Happify, Happpiness Trainer, and e-Positive Spin. Three of them are based on PP (all except Happiness Trainer). They can easily be found on the Internet.

1. *Uplifted* is an online game in which players answer questions to become more positive. At the first level, a little doll is helped on its way to the fictional land of the Happ. This game encourages players to reflect on what brightens their world. After players navigate the platforms in each level, *Uplifted* asks the players three questions about gratitude and positive experiences (i.e., "Who is the most important person in your life?" "What couldn't you live without?" and "What made you smile today?") and stores these answers for later recall. *Uplifted* highlights the positive aspects of the players' lives and rewards them for each challenge they overcome. *Uplifted* states, "Research in the field of Positive Psychology shows that cultivating optimism in this way can undo stress and can train the brain to become more optimistic and positive." Seventeen references are mentioned, of which ten are scientific articles.

2. *Happify* consists of several components, including online training courses. Each course starts with a separate heading "Why It Works" with referrals to several scientific studies. On their website (my.happify.com/research/), a comprehensive list is given. *Happify* offers courses, videos, texts, and exercises. They use the game *Uplift* (different from *Uplifted*) to train the brain to become more positive, and they mention the broaden-and-build theory in the section "Why It Works": "Accord-

ing to Professor Fredrickson, even temporary positive emotions like joy or interest can result in a 'broadening' of our thoughts, and actions, and help regulate our negative emotions."

3. *Happiness Trainer* is not supported by the theory of PP; according to the description it is based on Cognitive Bias Modification. The app states, "Current research in CBM (Cognitive Bias Modification) shows that through brain training, you can change a negative outlook to positive and thereby make yourself feel happier." No scientific source is mentioned, but the app seems to be based on a method similar to cognitive bias modification (see below), where smiling faces must be quickly selected from a list of sixteen faces with different expressions. *Happiness Trainer* seems to use a simplified form of CBM.

COGNITIVE BIAS MODIFICATION

Cognitive accounts of depression and anxiety disorders emphasize the importance of cognitive biases. For example, depression and other mood disturbances are characterized by negative interpretation biases, that is, a tendency to interpret information in a negative way. Depressed mood is also associated with a deficit in generating positive thoughts about the future. A cognitive bias modification (CBM) paradigm targeting both interpretation bias and positive imagery may therefore have particular potential in developing innovative treatments for depression (Holmes, Lang, & Deeprose, 2009).

Holmes and colleagues propose that negative intrusive imagery, a lack of positive imagery, and negative interpretation bias all
serve independently and interactively to maintain depressed mood.
Research (Blackwell & Holmes, 2010) shows preliminary evidence
for its effectiveness, paving the way for the development of a novel
online treatment for depression (Bannink, 2012).

---

4. *E-Positive Spin* aims to train people's ability to identify and associate
   positive events with positive feelings, enhancing their well-being and
   happiness. It is an online game in which an image (a certain facial
   expression) and a word (an emotion) are displayed. Players should specify as soon as possible whether the image and the word are a "match" or
   "no-match." The website states:

   There is increasing evidence that focusing on positive information
   boosts positive feelings and well-being, while attending to negative
   information makes you feel more stressed and vulnerable . . . . Training to tune into positive image–word associations will help build a
   cycle of positivity, and flow on effects to reducing stress and boosting
   well-being and resilience.

   The app lists three scientific studies: Fredrickson (2000), Isaacowitz
   (2005), and Tugade, Fredrickson, and Feldman Barrett (2004). In terms of
   theory, the app seems to be based on the broaden-and-build theory; how-

ever, in terms of method, it seems to be based on cognitive bias modification, although this is nowhere mentioned.

1. To complicate matters further, some apps refer to PP or other scientific
    studies but do not explicitly mention any research; these include, for
    example, apps with mindfulness applications. And there are apps that
    do not mention any PP research, although they use gratitude exercises.
2. In sum, OPPIs are promising interventions for supporting people in
    strengthening positive emotions. However, only a few OPPIs rely on
    research, mostly PP, such as the broaden-and-build-theory of positive
    emotions. A meta-analysis by Webb, Joseph, Yardley, and Michie (2010)
    shows that OPPIs are more effective when they are based on research.
3. Presently, much attention is being paid to *blended care*, in which reg-
    ular face-to-face interviews are combined with online psychothera-
    peutic interventions such as email, chats, online treatment modules,
    and online access to the client's personal health file. Several Internet
    interventions for common mental disorders have been developed and
    tested, and evidence shows that these treatments often result in out-
    comes similar to those for face-to-face psychotherapy and that they are
    cost-effective. Although treatments including guidance seem to lead to
    better outcomes than unguided treatments, this guidance can be mainly
    practical and supportive rather than explicitly therapeutic in orienta-
    tion. For OPPIs to achieve the positive effects that are often attained
    in guided self-care interventions, the possibilities of automated guid-
    ance should be further explored. In sum, there is now a large body of

evidence suggesting that Internet interventions work. Several research questions remain open, including how OPPIs can best be blended with traditional forms of care.

M-health

Together with e-health, *m-health* ensures that mental health services remain affordable and accessible for a wide audience. M-health means *mobile health*, available through smartphones and tablets. This allows clients to receive health care not only on their own time but also independent of where they are. According to Chang, Kaasinen, and Kaipainen (2013), these are promising devices for using OPPIs. There is preliminary evidence that the use of smartphone apps contributes to a better mood and more happiness (Parks, Della Porta, Pierce, Zilca, & Lyubomirsky, 2012).

In addition to the technology of OPPIs, the use of *robots* or *social agents* in (mental) health care offers new opportunities. Robots, for example, can apply PP applications with residents of a nursing home to increase their well-being. However, many steps are still necessary to get from "promising" to "proven to be effective."

Below, some OPPIs for smartphones and tablets are described. The provision of multiple OPPIs at the same time can provide variety and stimulate adherence.

1. *PsyMate* (Myin Germeys, Birchwood, & Kwapill, 2011) ensures that the smartphone gives a signal several times a day, at which point

some questions appear on the screen. The questions assess partic- ipants' mood at that moment (positive or negative affect) as well as their behavior and the environment in which they find themselves. On the basis of this information, the professional and the client together get a picture of the extent to which a certain characteristic, such as experiencing positive affect, occurs throughout the day. They also discover the degree to which this characteristic fluctuates as a function of behavior and context. For example, a client may notice that he is experiencing positive affect when physically active. Such observations may provide clues and encourage the client to exercise more. Research shows that in this way, participants generate more positive affect and reduce psychological symptoms (Kramer, 2014).

2. *Live Happy* (Lyubomirski, 2008) includes applications such as setting goals, keeping a gratitude journal on the smartphone, and visualizing "your best possible self" (see Application 67). Of the more than 3,000 people who downloaded the app, about 10 percent were found to have kept track of their mood. During the program, the mood and well-being of the participants improved, and a variety of applications increased the effect. It was striking that some participants preferred applications that were not shown to be effective, according to this research, such as set- ting goals and "Savor pleasant moments" (see Application 25).

Usually OPPIs are offered separately, however. Schueller and Parks (2012) researched using multiple OPPIs simultaneously. The purpose of their study was to investigate methods of dissemination that could increase the acceptability and effectiveness of PP exercises. To achieve this goal, they compared the use of PP exercises when delivered in packages of two, four, or six exercises. More than 1,300 self-help-seeking participants enrolled in this study by visiting an online research portal. Consenting participants were randomly assigned to receive two, four, or six positive psychology exercises (or assessments only) over a six-week period. Participants visited an automated website that distributed exercise instructions, provided email reminders, and contained the baseline and follow-up assessments. Following each exercise, participants rated their enjoyment of the exercise, answered how often they had used each technique, and completed outcome measures.

All conditions produced significant reductions in depressive symptoms; however, this reduction was larger in the groups that received two or four exercises compared with the six-exercise or control condition. Increasing the number of exercises presented to participants increased the use of the techniques and did not increase dropout. Participants may be more likely to use these skills when presented with a variety of options. Increasing the number of exercises delivered to participants produced a curvilinear relationship, with those in the two- and four-exercise conditions reporting larger decreases in depressive symptoms than participants in the six-exercise or control conditions. Although research generally offers a single exercise to test isolate effects, this study supports the premise that studying variability in dissemination can produce important findings.

Applications at a Glance

Chapter 1. Positive Psychology

1. Look for character strengths
2. Register character strengths
3. Talk about strengths
4. Create a strength roadmap
5. Notice what should not change
6. Observe better moments
7. List fifty positive things
8. Allow plants in the workplace
9. Put modesty aside
10. Look through a positive lens
11. Imagine a future with strengths
12. Celebrate strengths

13. Search for professional strengths
14. Find exceptions to the problem

Chapter 2. Positive Emotion

15. Ask what makes them happy
16. Increase creativity
17. Turn on positivity
18. Create a positive mood board
19. Think positive self-statements
20. Laugh (more)
21. Get a pet
22. Look at green
23. Be mindful
24. Design a beautiful day
25. Savor pleasant moments
26. Value time
27. Apply loving-kindness meditation
28. Focus on the taste of food
29. Use Wu Wei
30. List three blessings
31. List three funny things
32. Use a reminder
33. Collect champagne corks

34. Remember being at your best

35. Define special moments

36. Pay attention to what is good for you

37. Draw or paint moments of happiness

38. Write about an intensely positive experience

39. Keep a positive diary

40. Write down what you are grateful for

41. Write down what you are pleased about—despite what is happening or has happened

42. Practice self-compassion

43. Surround the anxious self in compassion

44. Observe compassionate moments

45. Become your own best friend

46. Discover self-compassion in the past

47. Find a safe place

48. Increase physical energy

49. Choose to be happy

50. Plan pleasurable activities

51. Relax

52. Design a daily ritual of joy

53. Focus on what works

54. Focus on useful or fun things

55. Apply the loci method

56. Listen to favorite music

57. Learn to play an instrument
58. Observe your mood
59. Challenge negative thoughts

Chapter 3. Engagement

60. Experience flow
61. Answer three questions to build happiness
62. Change a negative into a positive narrative
63. Formulate a goal
64. Scale progress
65. Create a cartoon
66. Use mental contrasting
67. Visualize a best possible self
68. Ask the miracle question
69. Write a letter from the future
70. Start at chapter two
71. Imagine an older and wiser version of yourself
72. Spend time with an older version of yourself
73. Thanks from your future self
74. Plan a vacation
75. Describe a year later
76. Create a five-year plan
77. Visualize the preferred future
78. Visualize the next signs of progress

79. Write a eulogy

80. Imagine an anniversary

81. Imagine winning a prize

82. Visit a curiosity shop

83. Work on personal growth

84. Gather experiences

85. Find a hobby

86. Develop a positive addiction

87. Choose the role of victim or survivor

88. Write four resolving letters

89. Show yourself respect

90. Play the what-if game

91. Ask about a difficult childhood

92. Write, read, and burn

93. Think of a ritual

94. Develop a shared ritual

95. Learn optimism

96. Increase optimism

97. Imagine the worst-case scenario

98. Imagine the best-case scenario

99. Choose the role of pessimist or optimist

Chapter 4. Relationships

100. Find strengths in the environment

101. Capitalize on positive events

102. Experience (more) love

103. Use honeymoon talk

104. Respond in an active-constructive way

105. Practice active listening

106. Celebrate relationships

107. Plan a strengths date

108. Observe what the other person is doing that is helpful

109. Spend quality time with friends

110. Reflect on social interactions

111. Create loving connections

112. Ensure connections at work or school

113. Create compassion in daily life

114. Eat together

115. Perform acts of kindness

116. Count acts of kindness

117. Do something new

118. Focus less on yourself

119. Give something you like

120. Do something unexpectedly positive

121. Surprise someone

122. Create positive paranoia

123. Give compliments

124. Use positive reinforcement

125. Communicate respectfully

126. Find connectedness

127. Find supporters

128. Make an accordion with compliments

129. Create an appreciation wall

130. Create a compliment box

131. Gossip positively

132. Use happiness detectives

133. Start with a positive opening

134. Hold positive meetings

135. Say "yes, and" instead of "yes, but"

136. Control anger

137. Apologize

138. Forgive

Chapter 5. Meaning

139. Find meaning

140. Use character strengths in a new way

141. Find meaning and purpose

142. Find meaning in the best, worst, and most ordinary events

143. Cross a river

144. Describe how you want to be remembered

145. Live in line with your values
146. Find self-worth
147. Find a kernel of positivity
148. Write a rainy day letter
149. Keep a gratitude journal
150. Make a gratitude visit
151. Write a thank-you note
152. Give thanks for the ordinary and the extraordinary
153. Be grateful in four steps
154. Count your blessings
155. Find balance in your complaining
156. Dwell on mortality and loss
157. Search for hope
158. Enhance hope
159. Ask questions about hope
160. Experiment with hope
161. Predict the next day
162. Answer four basic solution-focused questions
163. See hope as a journey
164. Find a glimmer of hope
165. Open a door
166. Develop hope at work
167. Build high-quality connections
168. Practice spirituality
169. Take care of your body

Chapter 6. Accomplishment

170. Perform five things for (more) success

171. Find positive differences

172. Identify success, talent, and ambition

173. Make a best self-portrait

174. Find previous successes

175. Make a success box

176. Pass on competencies

177. Make a certificate of competence

178. Turn around the 80-20 deficit rule

179. Savor successful memories

180. Start a positive conversation at work

181. Write how you are doing in ten years

182. Celebrate success

183. Create a success certificate

184. Report sparkling moments

185. Collect proof of competence

186. Listen with strength ears

187. Maximize success

188. Discuss the most challenging case

189. Interview about success

190. Feel proud

191. Ask what they take home

192. View the problem from a different perspective

193. Persevere

194. Do something else

195. Practice for the *Guinness World Records*

196. Build a growth mindset

197. Encourage a growth mindset

198. Opt for better

199. Request feedback

200. Think of solutions

201. Observe your idol

References

Affleck, G., Tennen, H., Croog, S., & Levine, S. (1987). Causal attribution, perceived benefits, and morbidity after a heart attack: An 8-year study. *Journal of Consulting and Clinical Psychology, 55*(1), 29–35.

Ai, A. L., Cascio, T., Santangelo, L. K., & Evans-Campbell, T. (2005). Hope, meaning, and growth following the September 11, 2001 terrorist attacks. *Journal of Interpersonal Violence*, 20, 5, 523-548.

Aknin, L. B., & Human, L. J. (2015). Give a piece of you: Gifts that reflect givers promote closeness. *Journal of Experimental Social Psychology, 60,* 8–16.

Allemand, M., Hill, P., Ghaemmaghami, P., & Martin, M. (2012). Forgivingness and subjective well-being in adulthood: The moderating role of future time perspective. *Journal of Research in Personality, 46,* 32–39.

Allen, R. E., & Allen, S. D. (1997). *Winnie-the-Pooh on success.* New York, NY: Dutton.

Aristotle. (1998). *Nicomachean ethics.* Mineola, NY: Dover.

Aron, A., Norman, C. C., Aron, E. N., McKenna, C., & Heyman, R. E. (2000), Couples' shared participation in novel and arousing activities and experienced relationship quality. *Journal of Personality and Social Psychology, 78,* 273–284.

Bakker, A. B., & Derks, D. (2010). Positive occupational health psychology. In S. Leka & J. Houdmont (Eds.), *Occupational health psychology: A key text.* Oxford, UK: Wiley.

Bakker, J. M., Bannink, F. P., & Macdonald, A. (2010). Solution-focused psychiatry. *The Psychiatrist, 34,* 297–300.

Bannink, F. P. (2007a). *Gelukkig zijn en geluk hebben* [On being happy and being lucky]. Amsterdam: Pearson.

Bannink, F. P. (2007b). Solution-focused brief therapy. *Journal of Contemporary Psychotherapy, 37*(2), 87–94.

Bannink, F. P. (2008a). Posttraumatic success: Solution-focused brief therapy. *Brief Treatment and Crisis Intervention, 7,* 1–11.

Bannink, F. P. (2008b). Solution-focused mediation. *Conflict Resolution Quarterly, 25*(2), 163–183.

Bannink, F. P. (2009). *Positieve psychologie in de praktijk* [Positive psychology in practice]. Amsterdam: Hogrefe.

Bannink, F. P. (2010a). *1001 solution-focused questions: Handbook for solution-focused interviewing.* New York, NY: Norton.

Bannink, F. P. (2010b). *Handbook of solution-focused conflict management.* Cambridge, MA: Hogrefe.

Bannink, F. P. (2010c). *Oplossingsgericht leidinggeven* [Solution-focused leadership]. Amsterdam: Pearson.

Bannink, F. P. (2012). *Practicing positive CBT: From reducing distress to building success.* Oxford, UK: Wiley.

Bannink, F. P. (2014a). Positive CBT. *Journal of Contemporary Psychotherapy, 44*(1), 1–8.

Bannink, F. P. (2014b). *Post traumatic success: Positive psychology and solution-focused strategies to help clients survive and thrive.* New York, NY: Norton.

Bannink, F. P. (2015a). *Handbook of positive supervision.* Cambridge, MA: Hogrefe.

Bannink, F.P. (2015b). *101 Solution-focused questions for help with: Vol. 1. Anxiety; Vol. 2. Depression; Vol. 3. Trauma.* New York, NY: Norton.

Bannink, F.P. (2016). *Positieve psychologie. De toepassingen* [Positive psychology. The applications]. Amsterdam, Netherlands: Boom.

Bannink, F. P., & Haan, R. den. (2016). *Beterweters. Van lastige naar optimale interacties in de (g)gz* [Know-it-alls. From difficult to optimal interactions in (mental) health care]. Amsterdam, Netherlands: Boom.

Bannink, F. P., & Jackson, P. Z. (2011). Positive psychology and solution focus: Looking at similarities and differences. *Interaction: The Journal of Solution Focus in Organisations, 3*(1), 8–20.

Barnard, L. K., & Curry, J. F. (2011). Self-compassion: Conceptualizations, correlates & interventions. *Review of General Psychology, 15,* 289–303.

Barrell, J. J., & Ryback, D. (2008). *Psychology of champions.* Westport, CT: Praeger.

Baumeister, R. F., & Vohs, K. D. (2005). The pursuit of meaningfulness in life. In C. R. Snyder & S. J. Lopez (Eds.), *Handbook of positive psychology* (pp. 608–618). New York, NY: Oxford University Press.

Beck, A. T., Weissman, A., Lester, D., & Trexles, L. (1974). The measurement of pessimism: The hopelessness scale. *Journal of Consulting and Clinical Psychology, 42,* 861–865.

Beck, J. S. (2011). *Cognitive behaviour therapy: Basics and beyond* (2nd ed.). New York, NY: Guilford.

Bellier-Teichmann, T., & Pomini, V. (2015). Evolving from clinical to positive psychology: Understanding and measuring patients' strengths: A pilot study. *Journal of Contemporary Psychotherapy, 45,* 99–108.

Berg, A. E. van den, & Winsum-Westra, M. van (2006). Ontwerpen met groen voor gezondheid [Design with the color green for health]. *Alterra-rapport 1371, Reeks Belevingsonderzoek 15.* Wageningen, Netherlands: Alterra.

Berk, L. S., & Tan, S. A. (1997). A positive emotion: The eustress metaphor, mirthful laughter modulates immune system immunocytes. San Francisco: p. S174/D010.

Blackwell, S. E., & Holmes, E. A. (2010). Modifying interpretation and imagination in clinical depression: A single case series using cognitive bias modification. *Applied Cognitive Psychology, 24*(3), 338–350.

Bode, C., & Arends, R. Y. (2013). Optimale ontwikkeling, persoonlijke doelen en zelfregulatie [Optimal development, personal goals, and self-regulation]. In E. Bohlmeijer, L. Bolier, G. Westerhof, & J. A. Walburg (Eds.), *Handboek positieve psychologie* [Handbook of positive psychology] (pp. 129–152). Amsterdam, Netherlands: Boom.

Boehm, J. K., Lyubomirsky, S., & Sheldon, K. S. (2011). A longitudinal experimental study comparing the effectiveness of happiness-enhancing strategies in Anglo Americans and Asian Americans. *Cognition & Emotions, 25,* 263–272.

Bohlmeijer, E., & Bannink, F. P. (2013). Posttraumatische groei [Posttraumatic growth]. In E. Bohlmeijer, L. Bolier, G. Westerhof, & J. Walburg (Eds.), *Handboek positieve psychologie* [Handbook of positive psychology] (pp. 211–227). Amsterdam, Netherlands: Boom.

Bolier, L. (2015). *Online positive psychology: Using the Internet to promote flourishing on a large scale.* Doctoral thesis, University Twente, the Netherlands.

Bolier, L., Walburg, J. A., & Boerefijn, J. (2013). Positieve psychologie op school [Positive psychology in education]. In E. Bohlmeijer, L. Bolier, G. Westerhof, & J. A. Walburg (Eds.), *Handboek positieve psychologie* [Handbook of positive psychology] (pp. 325–338). Amsterdam, Netherlands: Boom.

Bonanno, G. A., & Kettner, D. (1997). Facial expressions of emotion and the course of conjugal bereavement. *Journal of Abnormal Psychology, 106,* 126–137.

Bostwick, K. C. P. (2015). *The effectiveness of a malleable mindset intervention in an introductory psychology course.* Unpublished master's thesis, Oregon State University, Corvallis.

Brandtstädter, J., & Rothermund, K. (2002). The life-course dynamics of goal pursuit and goal adjustment: A two process framework. *Developmental Review, 22,* 117–150.

Branigan, C., Fredrickson, B. L., Mancuso, R. A., & Tugade, M. M. (2000). The undoing effect of positive emotions. *Motivation and Emotion, 24,* 237–258.

Bray, P. (2009). A broader framework for exploring the influence of spiritual experience in the wake of stressful life events: Examining connections between post-traumatic growth and psycho-spiritual transformation. *Mental Health, Religion & Culture, 13*(3). doi: 10.1080/13674670903367199

Buchanan, K. E., & Bardi, A. (2010). Acts of kindness and acts of novelty affect life satisfaction. *Journal of Social Psychology, 15*(3), 235–237.

Burns, G. W. (2001). *101 healing stories: Using metaphors in therapy.* New York, NY: Wiley.

Burton, C. M., & King, L. A. (2004). The health benefits of writing about intensely positive experiences. *Journal of Research in Personality, 38*(2), 150–163.

Bushman, B. J., Baumeister, R. F., & Stack, A. D. (1999). Catharsis, aggression, and persuasive influence: Self-fulfilling or self-defeating prophecies? *Journal of Personality and Social Psychology, 76,* 367–376.

Butler, J., & Kern, M. L. (2015). The PERMA Profiler: A brief multidimensional measure of flourishing. Retrieved from http://www.peggykern.org/questionnaires.html

Carroll, L. (1865). *Alice's adventures in wonderland.* New York, NY: Barnes & Noble.

Carver, C. S., Scheier, M. F., & Segerstrom, S. (2010). Optimism. *Clinical Psychology Review, 30,* 879–889.

Chang, T. R., Kaasinen, E., & Kaipainen, K. (2013). Persuasive design in mobile applications for mental well-being: Multidisciplinary expert review. In *Wireless mobile communication and healthcare* (pp. 154–162). Berlin, Germany: Springer.

Collins, A. (2014). Music education and the brain: What does it take to make a change? *Applications of Research in Music Education, 32*(2), 4–10.

Cooperrider, D. L., & Godwin, L. (2011). Positive organization development. In K. Cameron & G. Spreitzer (Eds.), *The Oxford handbook of positive organizational scholarship.* Oxford, UK: Oxford University Press.

Cooperrider, D. L., & Whitney, D. (2005). *Appreciative inquiry: A positive revolution to change.* San Francisco, CA: Berrett-Koehler.

Covey, S. R. (1989). *The seven habits of highly effective people.* New York, NY: Simon & Schuster.

Crumbaugh, J. C. (1971). Frankl's logotherapy: A new orientation in counseling. *Journal of Religion and Health, 10,* 373–386.

Csikszentmihalyi, M. (1990). *Flow: The psychology of optimal experience.* New York, NY: HarperCollins.

Danner, D. D., Snowdon, D. A., & Friesen, W. V. (2001). Positive emotions in early life and longevity: Findings from the nun study. *Journal of Personality and Social Psychology, 80*(5), 804–813.

Desmet, P. M. A., & Pohlmeijer, A. E. (2013). Positive design: An introduction to design for subjective well-being. *International Journal of Design, 7*(3), 5–19.

Diener, E., & Seligman, M. E. P. (2002). Very happy people. *Psychological Science, 13*(1), 81–84.

Diener, E., Suh, E. M., Lucas, R. E., & Smith, H. L. (1999). Subjective well-being: Three decades of progress. *Psychological Bulletin, 125,* 276–302.

Dijksterhuis, A. (2015). *Op naar geluk* [Towards happiness]. Amsterdam, Netherlands: Prometheus.

Dolan, Y. M. (1991). *Resolving sexual abuse.* New York, NY: Norton.

Dolan, Y. M. (1998). *One small step.* Watsonville, CA: Papier-Mache.

Drucker, P. F. (2002). *Managing in the next society.* New York, NY: Truman Talley.

Duckworth, A., & Gross, J.J. (2014). Self-control and grit: Related but separable determinants of success. *Current Directions in Psychological Science, 23*(5), 319–325.

Dweck, C. S. (2006). *Mindset: The new psychology of success.* New York, NY: Random House.

Einstein, A. (1954). *Ideas and opinions.* New York, NY: Crown.

Elliot, C. (2012). *Solution building in couples therapy.* New York, NY: Springer.

Emmons, R. A. (1997). Motives and goals. In R. Hogan & J. A. Johnson (Eds.), *Handbook of personality psychology* (pp. 485–512). San Diego, CA: Academic Press.

Emmons, R. A. (2003). Personal goals, life meaning, and virtue: Wellsprings of a positive life. In C. L. M. Keyes (Ed.), *Personality, identity, and character: Explorations in moral psychology* (pp. 256–270). New York, NY: Cambridge University Press.

Emmons, R. A. (2009). Greatest of the virtues? Gratitude and the grateful personality. In D. Narvaez & D. Lapsley (Eds.), *Personality, identity, and character: Explorations in moral psychology* (pp. 256–270). New York, NY: Cambridge University Press.

Emmons, R. A., & McCullough, M. E. (2003). Counting blessings versus burdens: An experimental investigation of gratitude and subjective well being in daily life. *Journal of Personality and Social Psychology, 84,* 377–389.

Emmons, R. A., & Shelton, C. M. (2005). Gratitude and the science of positive psychology. In C. R. Snyder & S. J. Lopez (Eds.), *Handbook of positive psychology* (pp. 459–471). New York, NY: Oxford University Press.

Flückiger, C., Caspar, F., Grosse Holtforth, M. C., & Willutzki, U. (2009). Working with patients' strengths: A microprocess approach. *Psychotherapy Research, 19*(2), 213–223.

Fowler, J. H., & Christakis, N. A. (2008). Dynamic spread of happiness in a large social network: Longitudinal analysis over 20 years in the Framingham Heart Study. *British Medical Journal, 337*(a2338), 1–9.

Frankl, V. E. (1963). *Man's search for meaning: An introduction to logotherapy.* Boston, MA: Beacon Press.

Fredrickson, B. L. (1998). What good are positive emotions? *Review of General Psychology, 2,* 300–319.

Fredrickson, B. L. (2000). Cultivating positive emotions to optimize health and well-being. *Prevention & Treatment, 3,* 0001a.

Fredrickson, B. L. (2001). The role of positive emotions in positive psychology: The broaden-and-build theory of positive emotions. *American Psychologist, 56*(3), 218. doi: 10.1037/0003-066X.56.3.218

Fredrickson, B. L. (2009). *Positivity.* New York, NY: Crown.

Fredrickson, B. L. (2013). *Love 2.0.* New York, NY: Hudson Street Press.

Fredrickson, B. L., & Branigan, C. (2005). Positive emotions broaden the scope of attention and thought-action repertoires. *Cognition and Emotion, 19,* 313–332.

Freud, S. (1928). Humor. *International Journal of Psychoanalysis, 9,* 1–6.

Froh, J. J., Sefick, W. J., & Emmons, R.A. (2008). Counting blessings in early adolescents: An experimental study of gratitude and subjective well-being. *Journal of School Psychology, 46,* 213–233.

Furman, B. (1998). *It is never too late to have a happy childhood.* London, UK: BT Press.

Gable, S. L., & Haidt, J. (2005). What (and why) is positive psychology? *Review of General Psychology, 9,* 103–110.

Gable, S. L., Reis, H. T., Impett, E. A., & Asher, E. R. (2004). What do you do when things go right? The intrapersonal and interpersonal benefits of sharing positive events. *Journal of Personality and Social Psychology, 87*(2), 228–245.

Gilbert, P. (2010). *Compassion focused therapy.* New York, NY: Routlegde.

Gladwell, M. (2008). *Outliers. The story of success.* New York, NY: Little, Brown.

Goldstein, N. J., Martin, S. J., & Cialdini, R. B. (2007). *Yes! 50 secrets from the science of persuasion.* London, UK: Profile Books.

Grant, A. M. (2003). The impact of life coaching on goal attainment, metacognition and mental health. *Social Behavior and Personality, 31,* 253–264.

Graybeal, C. (2001). Strengths-based social work assessment: Transforming the dominant paradigm. *Families in Society, 82(3),* 233–242.

Grotberg, E. H. (1995). *A guide to promoting resilience in children: Strengthening the human spirit.* The Hague, Netherlands: Bernard van Leer Foundation.

Hackmann, A., Bennett-Levy, J., & Holmes, E. A. (2011). *Oxford guide to imagery in cognitive therapy.* New York, NY: Oxford University Press.

Haybron, D. M. (2000). Two philosophical problems in the study of happiness. *Journal of Happiness Studies, 1,* 207–225.

Heath, C., & Heath, D. (2010). *Switch.* London, UK: Random House.

Hendrickx, F., & Bormans, L. (2015). *Hoop: The world book of hope.* Houten, Netherlands: TerraLannoo.

Hicks, J., Trent, J., Davis, W., & King, L. (2012). Positive affect, meaning in life, and future time perspective: An application of socioemotional selectivity theory. *Psychology and Aging, 27,* 181–189.

Histed, M. H., Pasupathy, A., & Miller, E. K. (2009). Learning substrates in the primary prefrontal cortex and striatum: Sustained activity related to successful actions. *Neuron, 63,* 244–253.

Hodges, T. D., & Asplund, J. (2010). Strengths development in the workplace. In P. Linley, S. A. Harrington, & N. Garcea (Eds.), *Oxford handbook of positive psychology at work.* Oxford, UK: Oxford University Press.

Holmes, E. A., Lang, T. A., & Deeprose, C. (2009). Mental imagery and emotion in treatments across disorders: Using the example of depression. *Cognitive Behaviour Therapy, 38,* 21–28.

Holt-Lunstad, J., Smith, T.B., & Layton, J.B. (2010). Social relationships and mortality risk: A meta-analytic review. PLoS Med 7 (7): e1000316. doi:10.1371/journal.pmed.1000316

Hoppmann, C., & Blanchard-Fields, F. (2010). Goals and everyday problem solving: Manipulating goal preferences in young and older adults. *Developmental Psychology, 46,* 1433–1443.

Isaacowitz, D. M. (2005). The gaze of the optimist. *Personality and Social Psychology Bulletin, 31*(3), 407–415.

Isaacowitz, D. M., Vaillant, G. E., & Seligman, M. E. P. (2003). Strengths and satisfaction across the adult lifespan. *International Journal of Ageing and Human Development, 57,* 181–201.

Isen, A. M. (2005). A role for neuropsychology in understanding the facilitating influence of positive affect on social behaviour and cognitive processes. In C. R. Snyder & S. J. Lopez (Eds.), *Handbook of positive psychology* (pp. 528–540). New York, NY: Oxford University Press.

Isen, A. M., Rosenzweig, A. S., & Young, M. J. (1991). The influence of positive affect on clinical problem solving. *Medical Decision Making, 11,* 221–227.

Jaarsma, T. A., Pool, G., Ranchor, A. V., & Sanderman, R. (2007). The concept and measurement of meaning in life in Dutch cancer patients. *Psycho-Oncology, 16,* 241–248.

Jong, P. de, & Berg, I. K. (2002). *Interviewing for solutions.* Belmint, CA: Thomson.

Kabat-Zinn, J. (1994). *Wherever you go there you are.* New York, NY: Hyperion.

Kashdan, T. B., Biswas-Diener, R., & King, L. A. (2008). Reconsidering happiness: The costs of distinguishing between hedonics and eudaimonia. *Journal of Positive Psychology, 3,* 219–233.

Kashdan, T. B., & McKnight, P. E. (2009). Origins of purpose in life: Refining our understanding of a life well lived. *Psychological Topics, 18*(2), 303–316.

Keyes, C. L. M. (1998). Social well-being. *Social Psychology Quarterly, 61,* 121–140.

Keyes, C. L. M. (2005). Mental illness and/or mental health? Investigating axioms of the complete state model of health. *Journal of Consulting and Clinical Psychology, 73,* 539–548.

Keyes, C. L. M., & Lopez, S. J. (2005). Toward a science of mental health. In C. R. Snyder & S. J. Lopez (2005), *Handbook of positive psychology* (pp. 45–59). New York, NY: Oxford University Press.

King, L. A. (2001). The health benefits of writing about life goals. *Personality and Social Psychology Bulletin, 27,* 798–807.

Kleiman, E. M., Adams, L. M., Kashdan, T. B., & Riskind, J. H. (2013). Gratitude and grit indirectly reduce risk of suicidal ideations by enhancing meaning in life: Evidence for a mediated moderation mode. *Journal of Research in Personality, 47*(5), 539–546.

Kramer, I. (2014). De experience-sampling-methode als toegevoegde behandeling van depressie: Een RTC [An experience-sampling-method as additional treatment of depression: An RTC]. *Tijdschrift voor Psychiatrie, 56*(6), 414–425.

Kranz, D., Bollinger, A., & Nilges, P. (2010). Chronic pain acceptance and affective well-being: A coping perspective. *European Journal of Pain, 14*(10), 1021–1025.

Kugle, S. (2007). *Sufis and saints' bodies: Mysticism, corporeality, and sacred power in Islam.* Chapel Hill: University of North Carolina Press.

Kuiper, E. C., & Bannink, F. P. (2012). Veerkracht. Bevorderen van veerkracht in de jeugdhulpverlening [Resilience. Promoting resilience in youthcare]. *Kind en Adolescent Praktijk, 3,* 134–139.

Kuiper, E. C., & Bannink, F. P. (2016). Veerkracht in jeugdhulpverlening en onderwijs [Promoting resilience in youthcare and education]. *Tijdschrift Positieve Psychologie, 2,* 59–64.

Lamers, S. M. A., Smit, A., & Hutschemaekers, G. J. M. (2013). Het meten van welbevinden en optimaal functioneren [Measuring well-being and optimal functioning]. In E. Bohlmeijer, L. Bolier, G. Westerhof, & J. A. Walburg (Eds.), *Handboek positieve psychologie* [Handbook of positive psychology] (pp. 387–397). Amsterdam, Netherlands: Boom.

Lazare, A. (2004). *On apology.* New York, NY: Oxford University Press.

Lewicki, R. J., & Wiethoff, C. (2000). Trust, trust development and trust repair. In M. Deutsch & P. T. Coleman (Eds.), *The handbook of conflict resolution.* San Francisco, CA: Jossey-Bass.

Lieberman, M. D., Eisenberger, N. I., Crockett, M. J., Tom, S. M., Pfeifer, J. H., & Way, B. M. (2007). Putting feelings into words. *Psychological Science, 18*(5), 421–428.

Linley, A. (2008). *Average to A+: Realising strengths in yourself and others.* Coventry, UK: CAPP Press.

Linley, P., Nielsen, K. M., Gillett, R., & Biswas-Diener, R. (2010). Using signature strengths in pursuit of goals: Effects on goal progress, need satisfaction, and well-being, and implications for coaching psychologists. *International Coaching Psychology Review, 5,* 6–15.

Litt, A. (2010). Lusting while loathing: Parallel counterdriving of wanting and liking. *Psychological Science, 21*(1), 118–125.

Lyubomirsky, S. (2008). *The how of happiness.* New York, NY: Penguin.

Lyubomirsky, S., King, L., & Diener, E. (2005). The benefits of frequent positive affect: Does happiness lead to success? *Psychological Bulletin of the American Psychological Association, 131*(6), 803–855.

Lyubomirsky, S., Sheldon, K. M., & Schkade, D. (2005). Pursuing happiness: The architecture of sustainable change. *Review of General Psychology, 9,* 111–131.

MacBeth, A., & Gumley, A. (2012). Exploring compassion: A meta-analysis of the association between self-compassion and psychopathology. *Clinical Psychology Review, 32,* 545–552.

MacIntyre, P., & Gregersen, T. (2012). Emotions that facilitate language learning: The positive-broadening power of the imagination. *Studies in Second Language Learning and Teaching, 2,* 193–213.

Macneil, A. J., Prater, D. L., & Busch, S. (2009). The effects of school culture and climate on student achievement. *Journal of Positive Psychology, 12,* 72–84.

Marx, G. (2002). *Groucho and me: The autobiography.* London, UK: Virgin.

Mascaro, N., & Rosen, D. H. (2008). Assessment of existential meaning and its longitudinal relations with depressive symptoms. *Journal of Social and Clinical Psychology, 27*(6), 576–599.

Maslow, A. (1970). *Motivation and emotion.* New York, NY: Harper & Row.

McCraty, R., Barrios-Choplin, B., Rozman, D., Atkinson, M., & Watkins, A. D. (1998). The impact of a new emotional self-management program on stress, emotions, heart rate variability, DHEA, and cortisol. *Integrative Physiological & Behavioral Science, 32*(2), 151–170.

McCullough, M. E., Kilpatrick, S. D., Emmons, R. A., & Larson, D. (2001). Is gratitude a moral affect? *Psychological Bulletin, 127,* 249–266.

Meevissen, Y., Peters, M., & Alberts, H. (2011). Become more optimistic by imagining a best possible self: Effects of a two week intervention. *Journal of Behavior Therapy and Experimental Psychiatry, 42,* 371–378.

Menninger, K. (1959). The academic lecture: Hope. *American Journal of Psychiatry, 12,* 481–491.

Meyers, M. C., Woerkom, M. van, & Bakker, A. B. (2013). The added value of the positive: A literature review of positive psychology interventions in organizations. *European Journal of Work and Organizational Psychology, 22*(5), 618–632.

Miller, T. (1995). *How to want what you have.* New York, NY: Avon.

Mitchell, J., Vella-Broderick, D., & Klein, B. (2010). Positive psychology and the Internet: A mental health opportunity. *Electronic Journal of Applied Psychology, 6*(2), 30–41.

Mongrain, M., & Anselmo-Matthews, T. (2012). Do positive psychology exercises work? A replication of Seligman et al. *Journal of Clinical Psychology, 68,* 382–389.

Myers, D. G. (2000). The funds, friends and faith of happy people. *American Psychologist, 55,* 56–67.

Myin Germeys, I., Birchwood, M., & Kwapill, T. (2011). From environment to therapy in psychosis: A real-world momentary assessment approach. *Schizophrenia Bulletin, 37*(2), 244–247.

Nakamura, J., & Csikszentmihalyi, M. (2005). The concept of flow. In C. R. Snyder & S. J. Lopez (Eds.), Handbook of positive psychology (pp. 89–105). New York, NY: Oxford University Press.

Neff, K. D. (2011). Self-compassion, self-esteem and well-being. *Social and Personality Psychology Compass, 5*(1), 1–12.

Neumann, J. von, & Morgenstern, O. (1944). *Theory of games and economic behavior.* Princeton, NJ: Princeton University Press.

Nolen-Hoeksema, S., & Davis, C.G. (2005). Positive responses to loss. In C. R. Snyder & S. J. Lopez (2005), *Handbook of positive psychology* (pp. 598–607). New York, NY: Oxford University Press.

Oettingen, G. (1999). Free fantasies about the future and the emergence of developmental goals. In J. Brandtstadter & R. M. Lerner (Eds.), *Action & self-development: Theory and research through the life span* (pp. 315–342). Thousand Oaks, CA: SAGE.

Oettingen, G., Hönig, G., & Gollwitzer, P. M. (2000). Effective self-regulation of goal attainment. *International Journal of Educational Research, 33,* 705–732.

O'Hanlon, B. (1999). *Evolving possibilities.* Philadelphia, PA: Brunner/Mazel.

Otake, K., Shimai, S., Tanaka-Matsumi, J., Otsui, K., & Fredrickson, B. L. (2006). Happy people become happier through kindness: A counting kindnesses intervention. *Journal of Happiness, 7,* 261–375.

Overholser, J. C. (1994). Elements of the Socratic method: III. Universal definitions. *Psychotherapy, 31,* 286–293.

Park, N., & Peterson, C. (2009). Strengths of character in schools. In R. Gilman, E. S. Huebner, & M. J. Furlong (Eds.), *Handbook of positive psychology in schools* (pp. 65–76). New York, NY: Routledge.

Parks, A. C., Della Porta, M. D., Pierce, R. S., Zilca, R., & Lyubomirsky, S. (2012). Pursuing happiness in everyday life: The characteristics and behaviors of online happiness seekers. *Emotion, 12,* 1222–1234.

Peacock, F. (2001). *Water the flowers, not the weeds.* Montreal, Quebec, Canada: Open Heart.

Peters, M. L., Rius-Ottenheim, N., & Giltay, E. J. (2013). Optimisme [Optimism]. In: E. Bohlmeijer, L. Bolier, G. Westerhof, & J. A. Walburg. *Handboek positi-*

eve psychologie [Handbook of positive psychology] (pp. 153–168). Amsterdam, Netherlands: Boom.

Peterson, C. (2006a). The values in action (VIA) classification of strengths. In M. Csikszentmihalyi & I. Csikszentmihalyi (Eds.), *A life worth living: Contributions to positive psychology* (pp. 29–48). New York, NY: Oxford University Press.

Peterson, C. (2006b). *A primer in positive psychology.* Oxford, UK: Oxford University Press.

Proctor, C., Maltby, J., & Linley, P. (2011). Strengths use as a predictor of well-being and health-related quality of life. *Journal of Happiness Studies, 12,* 153–169.

Proyer, R. T., Ruch, W., & Buschor, C. (2013). Testing strengths-based interventions: A preliminary study on the effectiveness of a program targeting curiosity, gratitude, hope, humor, and zest for enhancing life satisfaction. *Journal of Happiness Studies, 14,* 275–292.

Rashid, T. (2009). Positive intervention in clinical practice. *Journal of Clinical Psychology: In Session, 65*(5), 461–466.

Rath, T., & Conchie, B. (2008). *Strengths based leadership.* New York, NY: Gallup Press.

Reis, H. T., & Gable, S. L. (2003). Toward a positive psychology of relationships. In C. L. M. Keyes & J. Haidt (Eds.), *Flourishing: Positive psychology and the life well-lived* (pp. 129–160). Washington, DC: American Psychological Association.

Ritterband, L. M., Gonder-Frederick, L. A., Cox, D. J., Clifton, A. D., West, R. W., & Borowitz, S. M. (2003). Internet interventions: In review, in use, and into the future. *Professional Psychology: Research and Practice, 34,* 527–534.

Riva, G., Banos, R. M., Botella, C., Wiederhold, B. K., & Gaggioli, A. (2012). Positive technology: Using interactive technologies to promote positive functioning. *Cyberpsychology Behavior and Social Networking, 15,* 69–77.

Roeden, J. M., & Bannink, F. P. (2007). *Handboek oplossingsgericht werken met licht verstandelijk beperkte cliënten* [Handbook of solution-focused interviewing with clients with mild intellectual disabilities]. Amsterdam, Netherlands: Pearson.

Ryan, R. M., & Deci, E. L. (2001). On happiness and human potentials: A review of research on hedonic and eudemonic well-being. *Annual Review of Psychology, 52,* 141–166.

Ryan, R. M., & Huta, V. (2009). Wellness as health functioning or wellness as happiness: The importance of eudaimonic thinking. *Journal of Positive Psychology, 4,* 202–204.

Ryff, C. D. (1989). Happiness is everything, or is it? Explorations on the meaning of psychological well-being. *Journal of Personality and Social Psychology, 57,* 1069–1081.

Saleebey, D. (Ed.) (2007). *The strengths perspective in social work practice.* Boston, MA: Allyn & Bacon.

Scheier, M. F., & Carver, C. (1994). Distinguishing optimism from neuroticism: A reevaluation of the Life Orientation Test. *Journal of Personality and Social Psychology, 67,* 1063–1078.

Schueller, S. M., & Parks, A. C. (2012). Disseminating self-help: Positive psychology exercises in an online trial. *Journal of Medical Internet Research, 14*(3), e63. doi: 10.2196/jmir.1850

Seligman, M. E. P. (2002). *Authentic happiness.* London, UK: Brealey.

Seligman, M. E. P. (2005). Positive psychology, positive precention, and positive therapy. In *C. R. Snyder & S. J. Lopez (Eds.), Handbook of positive psychology (pp. 3–9). New York, NY: Oxford University Press.*

Seligman, M. E. P. (2011). *Flourish*. New York, NY: Free Press.

Seligman, M. E. P., & Csikszentmihalyi, M. (2000). Positive psychology: An introduction. *American Psychologist, 55*, 5–14.

Seligman, M. E. P., Steen, T. A., Park, N., & Peterson, C. (2005). Positive psychology progress: Empirical validation of interventions. *American Psychologist, 60*(5), 410–421.

Shazer, S. de (1985). *Keys to solution in brief therapy*. New York, NY: Norton.

Sheldon, K. M., Jose, P. E., Kashdan, T. B., & Jarden, A. (2015). Personality, effective goal-striving, and enhanced well-being: Comparing 10 candidate personality strengths. *Personality and Social Psychology Bulletin, 41*(4), 575–585.

Sheldon, K. M., & King, L. (2001). Why positive psychology is necessary. *American Psychologist, 56*(3), 216–217.

Simons, J., Vansteenkiste, M., Lens, W., & Lacante, M. (2004). Placing motivation and future time perspective theory in a temporal perspective. *Educational Psychology Review, 16*, 121–139.

Sin, N. L., Della Porta, M. D., & Lyubomirsky, S. (2011). Tailoring positive psychology interventions to treat depressed individuals. In S. I. Donaldson, M. Csikszentmihalyi, & J. Nakamura (Eds.), *Applied positive psychology: Improving everyday life, health, schools, work, and society* (pp. 79–96). New York, NY: Routledge.

Snyder, C. R. (1994). *The psychology of hope: You can get there from here*. New York, NY: Free Press.

Snyder, C. R. (2002). Hope theory: Rainbows in the mind. *Psychological Inquiry, 13*, 249–275.

Snyder, C. R., & Lopez, S. J. (2007). *Positive psychology: The scientific and practical explorations of human strengths*. Thousand Oaks, CA: Sage.

Snyder, C. R., Michael, S. T., & Cheavens, J. (1998). Hope as a psychotherapeutic foundation of common factors, placebos and expectancies. In M. A. Hubble, B. Duncan, & S. Miller (Eds.), *Heart and soul of change* (pp. 179–200). Washington, DC: American Psychological Association.

Stam, P., & Bannink, F.P. (2008). De oplossingsgerichte organisatie [The solution-focused organization]. *Tijdschrift VKJP, 35*(2), 62–72.

Susskind, L., & Cruikshank, J. L. (1987). *Breaking the impasse: Consensual approaches to resolving public disputes*. New York, NY: Basic Books.

Tamir, M., Mitchell, C., & Gross, J. J. (2008). Hedonic and instrumental motives in anger regulation. *Psychological Science, 19,* 324–328.

Tedeschi, R. G., & Calhoun, L. (2004). Posttraumatic growth: A new perspective on psychotraumatology. *Psychiatric Times, 21*(4), 1–8.

Tedeschi, R. G., & Calhoun, L. G. (2006). The posttraumatic growth inventory: Measuring the positive legacy of trauma. *Journal of Traumatic Stress, 9*(3), 455–471.

Tugade, M. M., Fredrickson, B. L., & Feldman Barrett, L. (2004). Psychological resilience and positive emotional granularity: Examining the benefits of positive emotions on coping and health. *Journal of Personality, 72*(6), 1161–1190.

Vaillant, G. E. (2002). *Aging well*. Boston, MA: Little, Brown.

Vallerand, R. J. (2015). *The psychology of passion*. New York, NY: Oxford University Press.

Veehof, M., Bohlmeijer, E., & Geschwind, N. (2013). Positieve emoties [Positive emotions]. In E. Bohlmeijer, L. Bolier, G. Westerhof, & J. A. Walburg (Eds.), *Handboek positieve psychologie* [Handbook of positive psychology] (pp. 105–122). Amsterdam, Netherlands: Boom.

Wansink, B., & Kleef, E. van (2014). Dinner rituals that correlate with child and adult BMI. *Obesity, 22*(5), 91–95.

Webb, T., Joseph, J., Yardley, L., & Michie, S. (2010). Using the Internet to promote health behavior change: A systematic review and meta-analysis of the impact of theoretical basis, use of behavior change techniques, and mode of delivery on efficacy. *Journal of Medical Internet Research, 12*(1), e4.

Westerhof, G. J., & Keyes, C. L. M. (2008). Geestelijke gezondheid is meer dan de afwezigheid van geestelijke ziekte [Mental health is more than mental illness]. *Maandblad Geestelijke volksgezondheid, 63,* 808–820.

Williams, A., & DeSteno, D. (2008). Pride and perseverance: The motivational role of pride. *Journal of Personality and Social Psychology, 94*(6), 1007–1017.

Wiseman, R. (2009). *59 seconds: Think a little change a lot.* London, UK: Pan Books.

Wong, P. T. P. (1998). Implicit theories of meaningful life and the development of the Personal Meaning Profile. In P. T. P. Wong & P. S. Fry (Eds.), *The human quest for meaning: A handbook of psychological research and clinical applications* (pp. 111–140). Mahwah, NJ: Lawrence Erlbaum.

Wong, P. T. P. (2014). Meaning in life. In A. C. Michalos (Ed.), *Encyclopedia of quality of life and well-being research* (pp. 3894–3898). New York, NY: Springer.

Wong, P. T. P., Wong, L. C. J., McDonald, M. J., & Klaassen, D. W. (Eds.) (2007). *The positive psychology of meaning and spirituality.* Abbotsford, BC: INPM Press.

Wood, A. M., Linley, P., Maltby, J., Kashdan, T. B., & Hurling, R. (2011). Using personal and psychological strengths leads to increases in well-being over time: A longitudinal study and the development of the strengths use questionnaire. *Personality and Individual Differences, 50,* 15–19.

World Health Organization. (2005). *Promoting mental health: Concepts, emerging evidence, practice.* Geneva, Switzerland.

Wrzesniewski, A., LoBuglio, N., Dutton, J. E., & Berg, J. M. (2013). Job crafting and cultivating positive meaning and identity in work. In A. B. Bakker (Ed.), *Advances in positive organizational psychology* (Vol. 1, pp. 281–302). London, UK: Emerald.

Young, S. (2009). *Solution-focused schools: Anti-bullying and beyond.* London, UK: BT Press.

Youssef, C. M., & Luthans, F. (2007). Positive organizational behaviour in the workplace: The impact of hope, optimism, and resiliency. *Journal of Management, 33,* 774–800.

Zika, S., & Chamberlain, K. (1992). On the relation between meaning in life and psychological well-being. *British Journal of Psychology, 83,* 133–145.

Websites

www.asfct.org

Association for the Quality Development of Solution Focused Consulting and Training (SFCT)

www.authentichappiness.sas.upenn.edu

Seligman with PP questionnaires

www.buildandshare.net

Exploring PP and narratives through model building with LEGO® materials

www.enpp.eu

Website European Network for Positive Psychology (ENPP)

www.fredrickson.socialpsychology.org

Fredrickson

www.fredrikebannink.com
Website of the author of this book

www.ggs.vic.edu.au
Geeling Grammar School

www.ippanetwork.org
International Positive Psychology Association (IPPA)

www.johnwheeler.co.uk
Wheeler

www.positran.fr
Boniwell

www.positivepsychology.org
Pennsylvania University

www.posttraumatic-success.com
Bannink's Post Traumatic Success

www.pos-cbt.com
Bannink's Positive CBT

www.solutionsdoc.co.uk
Macdonald, reseach solution-focused brief therapy

www.solworld.org
Solution Focus in Organisations (SOL)

www.strengthsfinder.com
Gallup

www.capp.co/R2StrengthsProfiler
R2 Strengths profiler

www.tandf.co.uk
The Journal of Positive Psychology

www.ted.com
Technology, Entertainment and Design (TED)

www.viacharacter.org
VIA survey of character strengths

www.youtube.com/watch?v=XLeUvZvuvAs
"The Power of Yet": The growth mindset

www.youtube.com/watch?v=oklOgZeEV7k
Bannink, author of this book

www.youtube.com/watch?v=7zOZbkJlxqc
Interview with Bannink on solution-focused brief therapy and PP at Norton

www.youtube.com/watch?v=_Cp-h5j5ry4
Bannink animation: "Post Traumatic Success"

https://www.youtube.com/watch?v=f8yMl0J7zCo
Bannink animation: "Building Success"

www.youtube.com/watch?v=oHv6vTKD6lg
"An Experiment in Gratitude"

Index

academic outcomes, optimism and, 112

acceptance, 160

accomplishment, 40, 194–224
  applications at a glance, 249–50
  focus on success and, 202–6
  growth mindset and, 218–24
  passion and grit and, 214–18
  in PERMA model, 7
  positive supervision and, 207–14
  see also goals and goal setting; success

accordion full of compliments, 143–44

action, positive *vs.* negative emotions and, 43

active-constructive responding, 128

active listening, practicing, 128–29

Adams, L. M., 10

adaptive attribution and explanation, 160

addiction
  lack of meaning and, 155
  pseudo-search for meaning and, 161

admiration, 46

adversity, gratitude and, 177

affection, 119

agency thinking, 179–80

aging well, Grant Study on, 5

AI. *see* Appreciative Inquiry (AI)

Alice's Adventures in Wonderland (Carroll), 84–85

Al-Shibli, 150

altruism, 7, 123
ambition, identifying, 199
amusement, 46
amygdala, 149
anger, controlling, 149
animal cartoon, goals and, 86–87
anniversary, imagining, 97
Anselmo-Matthews, T., 156
anxious self, surrounding with compassion, 64
apologizing, 149–50
appreciation of beauty and excellence, 14t, 153, 166–69
appreciation wall, creating, 144–45
Appreciative Inquiry (AI), 22–23, 31, 195, 203
approach goals, 76
apps, 238–39
Aristippus of Cyrene, 39
Aristotle, 79, 83, 101
Asplund, J., 22
attention, flow and, 81
attitude of gratitude, 171
autonomy, need for, 11
autotelic experience, 81
avoidance goals, 76
"away goals," athletes and, 30

Bakker, A. B., 22
Bandura, A., 194
Bannink, F. P., 20, 24, 203, 207
Barrell, J. J., 30
Basic Need Satisfaction Scale, 227
Baumeister, R. F., 153, 162, 165
beautiful day, designing, 53
beautiful in life reminder, 57
beauty, appreciation of, 14t, 153, 166–69
Beck, A. T., 179
Beck, J. S., 72
being at your best, remembering, 57–58
Berk, L. S., 50
best-case scenario, imagining, 114–15
best friend to yourself, becoming, 65
best possible self, visualizing, 90–91
best self-portrait, making, 199–200
better moments in life, observing, 18
Biondi, M., 115, 116, 117
Biswas-Diener, R., 9
Blake, W., 225
blame, positive, 84
blended care, 225, 237
blessings
    counting, 175, 177, 232
    writing down, 56
body, caring for, 192
Bolier, L., 231, 232, 233

Bollinger, A., 73
Bonanno, G. A., 189
boredom, addiction and, 161
Bostwick, K. C. P., 220
Branigan, C., 44
bravery, 12t
Bright Spots story, 31–32
broaden-and-build theory
 OPPIs and, 234, 236
 of positive emotions, 38, 42–44
Buddhism, 30
Build & Share method, 230
Buschor, C., 187

Calhoun, L., 102
capitalization, 17, 46, 119, 121, 214
capitalizing on positive events, 121
cardiac patients, hope, postoperative adjusting, and, 182
cards, 225
 for coaching or training purposes, 229
 in SQSS, 228, 229
careers, optimism and, 112
caring, 7
Carver, C., 112
car wash promotion, goals and, 85–86
CASP. *see* Control Autonomy Self-Realization and Pleasure Scale (CASP)

CBM. *see* Cognitive Bias Modification (CBM)
CBT. *see* cognitive behavior therapy (CBT)
celebrating relationships, 129
Certificate of Competence, making, 202
challenging case, discussing most challenging, 211–12
chameleon story, 36–37
champagne corks, collecting, 57
chance management, 203
chance managers, 203
Chang, T. R., 238
chapter two in your life story, starting at, 92
character strengths, 1, 8–18
 classification of, 12t–15t
 goal attainment, well-being and, 9–10
 looking for, 16
 noticing what should not change, 18
 reflecting on, 35
 registering, 16
 using in a new way, 157, 232
 see also strengths
chats, 237
Cheshire Cat conversation, unclear goals and, 84–85
Christakis, N. A., 130

chronic pain, well-being and, 73
Cialdini, R. B., 86
coaching, 225
cognitive behavior therapy (CBT), 72
Cognitive Bias Modification (CBM), 235–36, 237
cognitive coping, 182–83
collections, starting, 101
Collins, A., 71
common humanity, vs. isolation, 63
communication, respectful, 142
community, 8
compassion, 62
    Buddhist tale of, 65–66
    creating in daily life, 135–36
    spirituality and, 191
    surrounding the anxious self in, 64
    see also self-compassion
compassionate moments, observing, 65
competence
    collecting proof of, 209
    finding, in positive supervision, 207
    need for, 11
    questions, 200
    strengths and, 15
competencies, passing on, 201
complaining, finding balance in, 178

compliment box, 145, 200
compliments
    giving, 139–40
    make an accordion with, 143–44
connectedness, finding, 112–13. see also relationships
connections
    with compassion, 135–36
    eating together, 136
    ensuring at work or school, 134–35
    high-quality, 189–90
    performing acts of kindness, 136–37
    spirituality and, 191
constructive journalism, 28–29
contribution, spirituality and, 191
Control Autonomy Self-Realization and Pleasure Scale (CASP), 227
coping
    cognitive, 182–83
    effective, meaning and, 160
cortisol, negative emotions and level of, 150
counting your blessings, 175, 177
courage, x
    character strengths related to, 12t–13t, 214–15
Covey, S. R., 97

creativity, 12*t*, 44–47

crisis, solution-focused approach to, 70–71

cross a river application, trauma survival and, 159–60

Cruikshank, J. L., 124

Csikszentmihalyi, M., 2, 29, 39, 80

culture, optimism and, 113

curiosity, 9, 12*t*
  Nepalese children and, 26
  well-being and, 10

dance, joyful, 68

Davis, C. G., 167

deficit rule, 23

deliberate practice, 216, 217

depression, gratitude applications and, cautionary note, 171

describing a year later, 95

describing how you want to be remembered, 161

Design, in 4D cycle, 23

Desmet, P. M. A., 27

despair
  hope and, 180–81
  suicide and, 179

Destiny, in 4D cycle, 23

diagnosis, hopeful, 187

Diagnostic and Statistical Manual of Mental Disorders (DSM), 11

diary, positive, 59–62

Diener, E., 120, 130, 196

difficult childhood, asking about, 108

digressive narratives, 83

direct compliment, 139, 140

Discover, in 4D cycle, 23

dog I feed the most story, 74

Dolan, Y. M., 105, 106

dopamine levels, positive emotions and, 43

do something else, 217–18

drawing moments of happiness, 59

Dream, in 4D cycle, 23

Drucker, P. F., 24, 202

DSM. see Diagnostic and Statistical Manual of Mental Disorders (DSM)

Duckworth, A., 215

Dweck, C. S., 218, 219

eating together, 136

Edison, T., 215

education, positive psychology in, 25–26

efficacy, need for sense of, 165

e-health (electronic health), 225, 231–38

80-20 deficit-rule
  Appreciative Inquiry and, 195
  supervision and use of, 207
  turning around, 23–24, 204
Einstein, A., 87, 112, 217
Eliot, G., 78
email, 237
Emmons, R. A., 153, 177
emotional regulation, overidentification
  vs., 63
emotional well-being, 8
emotions, labeling, 149
empathy, love and, 123
employees, positive psychology and, 21,
  22
encouragement, 142
energy, strengths and, 15
engagement, 40, 78–117
  applications at a glance, 244–45
  defined, 78
  eudemonia and, 79
  flow and, 80–82
  goal setting and, 78–79, 82–87
  job crafting and, 21
  optimism and, 111–17
  in PERMA model, 7
  personal growth and, 99–101
  positive imagery and, 87–99
  posttraumatic growth and, 102–11
enjoyable experiences, pleasurable experiences vs., 39
enjoyment, asking clients about, 41
environment, finding strengths in,
  120–21
Epictetus, 167
Epicureans, 40
E-Positive Spin, 230, 236–38
eudemonia, 79
eudemonic perspective, quality of life
  and, 158
eulogy, writing, 96–97
excellence
  appreciation of, 14*t*, 166
  habit of, 101
exceptions to the problem, finding,
  35–36
experiencing, gathering, 100
explanatory style, 116
extraordinary events, giving thanks for,
  174

fairness, 13*t*
fear, 76
feedback, requesting, 223

feeling proud, 212–13

Feldman Barrett, L., 236

fight-or-flight (or freeze) response, 43

five-year plan, creating, 95–96

fixed mindset

  defined, 219

  growth mindset vs., 221t

Flourishing Scale, 227

flow, x, 11

  characteristics of, 80–81

  defined, 78

  description of, 29–30

  experiencing, 81

focus less on yourself, 138

food, focus on taste of, 55

forgiveness, 14t, 150

4D cycle: Discover, Dream, Design, and Destiny, 23

Fowler, J. H., 130

Frankl, V., 154, 155, 164

Fredrickson, B. L., 38, 43, 44, 45, 46, 62, 122, 123, 135, 137, 180, 235, 236

Freud, S., 72, 188

friendships, 119, 130–51, 132

fulfillment, 7, 162

fun, relationships and, 119

funny things list, 56–57

fun things, focus on, 69

Furman, B., 107

future, letter from, 92

future self, thanks from, 94

Gable, S. L., 119, 120, 127, 176

Gallup leadership study, 24

games, online, 230, 234

game theory, 124, 126

Geelong Grammar School (Australia), 26

geese, what we can learn from, 141–42

Ghandi, Mahatma, 118

Gilbert, P., 62

Gillett, R., 9

giving something you like, 138

goal formulation, in positive supervision, 207

goals and goal setting, 7, 239

  approach vs. avoidance and, 76

  Aristotle on, 83

  benefits with, 195–96

  best possible self and, 90–91

  character strengths and, 9–10

  engagement and, 78–79, 82–87

  formulating, 84

  gratitude and, 170

goals and goal setting (*continued*)
  happiness and, 195
  hope theory and, 179–80
  Live Happy and, 239
  mental contrasting and, 88–89
  positive imagery and, 87
  progress scale and, 85
  purpose and, 162
  stretch goals, 180
  success and, 197
  toward and away, 30
  visiting an imaginary shop, 98–99
  working toward, 163–64
Goldstein, N. J., 86
Gollwitzer, P. M., 88
good for you daily events, paying attention to, 58–59
good life
  Aristotle's idea of, 79
  basis of, 78, 80
  goal setting and, 82
gossip positively, 145–46
GQ-6. *see* Gratitude Questionnaire (GQ-6)
Grant, A. M., 59
Grant, W. T., 5
Grant Study, 5, 120

gratefulness, 169
  for being able to be grateful, 176
  four steps to, 174–75
  writing about, 61
gratitude, x, 10, 14*t*, 16, 18, 62, 153, 166, 169–78
  attitude of, 171
  daily gratitude groups, 170–71
  defined, 169
  indebtedness *vs.*, 170
  research results on, 171–72
  state, 169
  trait, 169
gratitude journals
  benefits of, 170
  keeping, 172
Gratitude Questionnaire (GQ-6), 228
Gratitude restaurant, San Francisco, 175
gratitude visit, making, 172–73
Graybeal, C., 226
Greeks, ancient, 40, 188
green color, soft fascination and, 51–52
grit, 10, 195, 214–18
  idol's success and, 224
  self-control *vs.*, 216
Gross, J. J., 75, 215

growth mindset, 48, 99, 195, 216, 217, 218–24
   academic success and, 220–21
   building, 221–22
   defined, 218
   encouraging, 222
   fixed mindset *vs.*, 221*t*
   misconceptions about, 219–20
   opting for better with, 222–23
Guinness World Records, practice for, 218

habits, defined, 101
"halo effect," holiday mindset and, 94–95
Happify, 234–35
happiness, 20, 231
   asking clients about, 41
   building, three questions for, 81–82
   choosing, 67
   contagious quality of, 130
   drawing or painting moments of, 59
   friendships and, 130
   good life and, 79
   love and, 123
   meaning and, 7
   optimism and, 79, 112
   positive design and, 27
   positive relationships and, 119–20

   spirituality and, 191
   working toward a goal and, 163, 195
happiness detectives, using, 146
happiness theory, 11
Happiness Trainer, 235
harmonious passion, 215
Haybron, D. M., 159
health, 30
   friendships and, 130, 131
   hope and, 178
   love and, 123
   optimism and, 112
   see also immune system; well-being
heart disease, OPPIs and recovery from, 233
hedonism, 39
high-quality connections, building, 189–90
hobbies, finding, 100–101
Hodges, T. D., 22
holiday mindset, positive emotions and, 94–95
Holmes, E. A., 236
honesty, 13*t*
honeymoon talk, 126–28
   four ways of responding with, 128
   team and, 127

Hönig, G., 88
hope, x, 14t, 46, 62, 153, 160, 166,
    178–88
  defined, 178–79
  despair and, 180–81
  enhancing, 181–83
  experiment with, 184
  finding glimmer of, 186
  searching for, 181
  seeing as a journey, 185–86
  solution-focused questions about,
    183–84, 185
  at work, developing, 188
hopeful diagnosis, 187
hopelessness, defined, 179
Hope Scale (HS), 228
hope theory, 185
HS. see Hope Scale (HS)
humanity, character strengths related
    to, 13t
humility, 14t
humor, 15t, 46, 50–51, 153, 166, 184,
    188–99. see also laughter
Huta, V., 158
Hutschemaekers, G. J. M., 227

idols, observing, 223–24
imagery, positive, 38

imaginary shop, visiting, 98–99
imagination, Einstein on, 87–88
immune system
  anger and, 150
  humor and, 189
  positive emotions and, 46–47
  see also health
indebtedness, gratitude vs., 170
indirect compliment, 140
inspiration, 46
Inspiration Scale (IS), 228
interest, 46
Internet
  PP interventions and, 225
  self-help courses on, 226
intimacy, 119
IS. see Inspiration Scale (IS)
Isaacowitz, D. M., 120, 236
Isen, A. M., 49
isolation, common humanity vs.,
    63

Jackson, P. Z., 20
Jarden, A., 9
Jesus Christ, 182
job crafting, 21
Jose, P. E., 9
Joseph, J., 237

journaling, positive, 38, 59–62
journalism, positive psychology and, 28–29
joy, 46
  designing daily ritual of, 68
  e-health programs and, 231
judgment, 12t
justice, character strengths related to, 13t– 14t

Kaasinen, E., 238
Kaipainen, K., 238
Kashdan, T. B., 9, 10
Keltner, D., 189
Keyes, C. L. M., 2
kindness, 13t
  counting acts of, 137
  performing acts of, 136–37
  for self, 62
King, L. A., 90, 196, 206
King, Martin Luther, Jr., 182
Kleef. E. van, 136
Kleiman, E. M., 10
Klein, B., 232
Kranz, D., 73

labeling, anger control and, 149
Lamers, S. M. A., 227

LAP-R. *see* Life Attitude Profile Revised (LAP-R)
laughter, 50–51, 184. *see also* humor
Lazare, A., 149
leadership, 14t
  solution-focused, 24–25
learned helplessness, 4, 111
learned optimism, 111, 113
learning, love of, 12t
LEGO® play, *Build & Share* method and, 230
Lester, D., 179
letter from the future, 92
Lewicki, R. J., 124
Lieberman, M. D., 149
Life Attitude Profile Revised (LAP-R), 228
life description, fully living out goals and, 161
life goals, purpose and, 162–63. *see also* goals and goal setting
Life Purpose Questionnaire (LPQ), 228
life story, starting at chapter two in, 92
liking, wanting *vs.*, 40–41
limbic system, 40
Linley, A., 15
Linley, P., 9, 15
listening, active, 128–29
Litt, A., 41

Live Happy, 239
loci method, applying, 69–70
logotherapy, 155–56
Lopez, S. J., 2, 158
loss, dwelling on, 178
love, 13*t*, 46, 122–30
    experiencing more of, 126
    of learning, 12*t*
    as "our supreme emotion," 122
loving connections, creating, 134
loving-kindness meditation, applying,
    54–55
LPQ. *see* Life Purpose Questionnaire
    (LPQ)
Lyubomirsky, S., 136, 163, 195, 196

MAAS. *see* Mindful Attention Awareness
    Scale (MAAS)
manifest strengths, potential strengths
    vs., 15–16
Martin, S. J., 86
Marx, G., 44
Mascaro, N., 160
Maslow, A., 169
meaning, 40, 152–93
    addiction and pseudo-search for, 161
    applications at a glance, 247–49
    appreciation of beauty and, 166–69

connection as essence of, 153–54
efficacy and, 165
finding, 157–58
finding in the best, worst, and most
    ordinary events, 158–59
four basic needs and quest for, 153,
    163
gratitude and, 169–78
hope and, 178–88
humor and playfulness and, 188–90
logotherapy and, 155–56
in PERMA model, 7
purpose and, 162–64
self-worth and, 165–66
spirituality and, 190–93
transcendence and, 166
values and, 164–65
will to live and, 160
see also purpose
meaningful life, four main needs and
    quest for, 152–53, 154, 162–66
Meaning in Life Questionnaire (MLQ),
    228
Meaning in Suffering Test (MIST), 228
meditation
    flow and, 81
    loving-kindness, 54–55
    mindful, 52

meetings, positive openings for start of, 146–47

memories, savoring successful ones, 205

Menninger, K., 178, 179

mental contrasting, 88–89

mental health
indicators of, x
meaning and, 158
well-being and, 2

Mental Health Continuum--Short Form (MHC SF), 228

mercy, 151

Meyers, M. C., 22

MHC SF. *see* Mental Health Continuum--Short Form (MHC SF)

m-Health (mobile health), 226, 238–40

Michie, S., 237

Miller, T., 174

Mindful Attention Awareness Scale (MAAS), 228

mindfulness, 38, 52–55
defined, 52
positive emotions and, 52–55
practicing, 52

mindfulness meditation, 149

mindset
defined, 218
fixed *vs.* growth, 221*t*

miracle question, asking, 91–92

MIST. *see* Meaning in Suffering Test (MIST)

Mitchell, C., 75

Mitchell, J., 232

MLQ. *see* Meaning in Life Questionnaire (MLQ)

modesty, putting aside, 32–33

Mongrain, M., 156

mood, observing, 73

mortality
dwelling on, 178
positive emotion and, 47

Moses, 182

motivation, goal attainment and, 179

mourners, humor and, 189

Muhammad, 182

music, listening to, 70–71

musical instruments, learning to play, 71

mutual trust, oxytocin and, 126

Nakamura, J., 80

narratives, types of, 83

National Center on Addiction and Substance Abuse (Columbia University), 161

Neff, K. D., 63

negative affect, positive affect balanced
    with, 72–77
negative emotions, 42
    action and, 43
    cortisol level and, 150
    decreasing, 73
    positive emotions balanced with, 38–39
    purpose of, 72
    undoing effects of, 45–46
    "yes, but," and, 148
negative narratives, changing into posi-
    tive narratives, 83–84
negative self-statements, 49t
negative thoughts, challenging, 74–76.
    see also pessimism
negotiation study positive affect in, 50
Nepalese children, curiosity and, 26
neuromuscular disease, gratitude and
    sample of adults with, 171
new things, doing, 137
next day prediction, 184–85
Nielsen, K. M., 9
Nietzsche, F., 152
Nikki principle, birth of, 4
Nilges, P., 73
9/11, mental health and hope in wake
    of, 182

Nolen-Hoeksema, S., 167
nun study, 47

obsessive passion, 215
Oettingen, G., 88
O'Hanlon, B., 191
older and wiser version of yourself
    imagining, 93–94
    spending time with, 94
Olympic gold medals, optimism and,
    115–17
one-time ritual, 109
online games, 230, 234
online interventions, defined, 231
online positive psychology interventions
    (OPPIs)
    effectiveness of, research on, 232–33,
        237–38
    E-Positive Spin, 236–38
    Happify, 234–35
    Happiness Trainer, 235
    simultaneous use of, 239–40
    Uplifted, 234
online treatment modules, 237
open a door intervention, 187–88
OPPIs. see online positive psychology
    interventions (OPPIs)

optimism, x, 38, 111–17
  benefits of, 112
  cultivating in *Uplifted* online game, 234
  finding significance after loss and, 167
  happiness and, 112
  increasing, 114
  learned, 111, 113
  visualizing preferred future and, 96
  writing toward, 113–14
optimist, choosing role of, 115
ordinary events, giving thanks for, 174
Otake, K., 137
Otsui, K., 137
Overholser, J. C., 164
overidentification, emotional regulation
  vs., 63
oxytocin
  love and, 123
  mutual trust and, 126

painting moments of happiness, 59
PANAS. *see* Positive and Negative Affect
  Schedule (PANAS)
Park, N., 4
Parks, A. C., 239
partnerships, observing helpful aspects
  of, 129–30

passion, 214–18
  success and, 195
  types of, 215
pathway thinking, 179
Peacock, F., 122
performing life, 3, 4, 194
PERMA. *see* positive emotion, engagement, relationships, meaning, and
  accomplishment (PERMA)
PERMA-Profiler, 8
perseverance, 13*t,* 195, 214, 216–17
persistence, 215, 216
personal fulfillment, engagement and,
  78
personal growth
  forms of, 99–100
  well-being and, 82
  work on, 100
Personal Growth Initiative Scale (PGIS),
  228
personal meaning, defining, 158
Personal Meaning Profile (PMP), 160
perspective, 12*t*
pessimism, 111, 112, 113
pessimist, choosing role of, 115
Peterson, C., 4, 120
pets, 51

PGIS. *see* Personal Growth Initiative Scale (PGIS)

physical energy, increasing, 67

PIL. *see* Purpose in Life Test (PIL)

pioneer story, what you give is what you get in, 133–34

plants in the workplace, 25

playfulness, 153, 166, 188–99. *see also* humor; joy; laughter

pleasant moments, savoring, 53, 239

pleasurable activities, planning, 68

pleasurable experiences, enjoyable experiences *vs.*, 39

pleasure
in itself, depression and, 39
worthwhile achievement and, 159

PMP. *see* Personal Meaning Profile (PMP)

Pohlmeijer, A. E., 27

political turmoil, hope and, 182

positive addictions, developing, 101

positive affect
interpersonal interactions and, 49
negative affect balanced with, 72–77
in negotiation study, 50

Positive and Negative Affect Schedule (PANAS), 227, 228

positive blame, 84

positive cognitive behavioral therapy, 20, 114

positive conversations at work, starting, 205

positive design, 27

positive deviance, 30–31

positive differences, finding, 197–98

positive emotion, engagement, relationships, meaning, and accomplishment (PERMA), xi, 1, 158

positive emotions, 38–77, 88, 160
action and, 43
amplifying, x
applications at a glance, 242–44
balance between positive and negative affect, 72–77
broaden-and build theory of, 38, 42–44
creativity and, 44–47
flow and, 80
goal setting and, 82
gratitude and, 177
immune system and, 46–47
increasing, 72–73
mindfulness and, 52–55
negative emotions balanced with, 38–39
in PERMA model, 6

playfulness and, 189
positive imagery and, 56–59
positive journaling and, 59–62
power of, 50
self-compassion and, 62–71
success and, 196
positive events
    capitalizing on, 121
    sharing, 17
positive gossip, 145–46
positive imagery, 38, 56–59
    engagement and, 78–79, 87–99
    uses for, 87
positive journaling, 38, 59–62
positive lens, looking through, 33–34
positive meetings, holding, 147
positive mental health, questionnaires
    for measuring, 227
positive mood board, creating, 48
positive narratives, negative narratives
    changed into, 83–84
positive paranoia, creating, 139
positive psychology (PP)
    applications at a glance, 241–42
    apps being developed for, 226
    character strengths in, 8–11, 12t–15t,
    15–18
    definitions of, 2

education and, 25–26
"family members" in domain of, x
focus of, ix
founders of, 2
journalism and, 28–29
online applications of, 225
psychology and psychiatry and,
    19–21
short history of, 3–5
society and, 30–36
sports and, 29–30
technology and, 27–28
underlying message of, 1
well-being theory in, 6–8
workplace and, 21–25
positive reinforcement, using, 140
positive relationships, 119, 132
positive school climate, criteria for,
    25–26
positive self-image, goal setting and, 82
positive self-statements, 34–35, 48, 49t
positive supervision, 195, 207–14
    four pillars of, 207
    strengths as focus in, 208–9
positive technology, 27
positive things list, 18
positive thinking, 231. *see also* optimism
positive time travel, 56

positivity
  finding kernel of, 168
  turning on, 47–48
positivity resonance, 123, 135
Posttraumatic Growth Inventory, 102
posttraumatic growth (PTG), 100,
  102–11
  caveats on, 103
  resilience and, 107
  shattered vase metaphor and, 110–11
posttraumatic success, 104, 168
posttraumatic success certificate, creating, 206
potential strengths, manifest strengths
  vs., 15–16
"Power of Yet, The," 219
PP. see positive psychology (PP)
PP interventions (PPIs), via smartphones, 225. see also online positive
  psychology interventions (OPPIs)
prayer, flow and, 81
predict the next day, 184–85
preferred future
  best possible self and, 90–91
  mental contrasting and, 88–89
  miracle question and, 91–92
  positive imagery of, 88
  visualizing, 96

preventive coping, 160
pride, 46, 212–13
prisoners' dilemma, 124–25
prize winning, imagining, 97–98
problems
  finding exceptions to, 35–36
  viewing from different perspective,
  214
problem solving, Appreciative Inquiry
  vs., 23
professional strengths, searching for,
  35
progress, visualizing next signs of, 96
progressive narratives, 83
progress scale, 85
Proyer, R. T., 187
prudence, 14t
psychoeducation, online interventions
  and, 231
psychological well-being, 8
Psychological Well-Being Scale, 227
psychotherapy
  for posttraumatic success, 20
  strength-perspective used in, 20–21
Psyfit, research results on, 232–33
PsyMate, 238–39
PTG. see posttraumatic growth (PTG)
PTSD, 103, 170

purpose, 8
  defined, 162
  finding, 157–58
  goals *vs.*, 163
  need for, 162–63
  will to live and, 160
  see also meaning
Purpose in Life Test (PIL), 228

Quality of Life Inventory (QOLI), 228
quality time, with friends, 132
questionnaires, 225, 226–28

Rainy Day Letter, writing, 168–69
Rapid Fire Facts, 74
Rashid, T., 20
reciprocity, mutual trust and, 124
Recovery, Resilience, and enRichment,
    posttraumatic success and, 104
reflection, in positive supervision,
    207
Reis, H. T., 119
relatedness, need for, 11
relationships, 40, 118–51
  applications at a glance, 246–47
  celebrating, 129
  friendship, 130–51
  gratitude in, 176

love in, 122–30
in PERMA model, 7
positive, 119, 132
relaxation, 68
religion, 190
resilience, x, 10, 62
  gratitude and, 177
  job crafting and, 21
  love and, 123
  meaning in life and, 154
  positive emotions and, 45
  posttraumatic growth and, 107
  3 Cs of spirituality and, 191
resolving letters, writing, 106
respect, showing for yourself, 107
respectful communication, 142
reverse mental contrasting, 89
Riskind, J. H., 10
risk management, 203
Ritterband, L. M., 231
rituals
  shared, 110
  thinking of, 109–10
robots, 28, 238
Romans, ancient, 192
Rosen, D. H., 160
R2 Strengths Profiler, 11, 15–16, 227
Ruch, W., 187

Ryan, R. M., 158
Ryff, C. D., 119

sadness, contagious quality of, 130–31
safe place, finding, 67
sailboat analogy, positivity/negativity
    dynamic and, 76–77
Save the Children, 31
savoring pleasant moments, 53
Scheier, M. F., 112
Schkade, D., 136
schools
    ensuring connections in, 134–35
    happiness detectives in, 146
    positive, 25–26
Schopenhauer, A., 72
Schueller, S. M., 239
SCS. *see* Self-Compassion Scale (SCS)
Seeking of Noetic Goals (SONG), 228
self-actualization, gratitude and, 169
self-care, 192
self-compassion, 38, 62–71, 231
    benefits of, 63
    discovering in the past, 66
    practicing, 64
    see also compassion
Self-Compassion Scale (SCS), 63, 228
self-confidence, character strengths and, 9

self-control
    forgiveness and, 150
    grit *vs.*, 216
self-determination theory, 11
self-efficacy, success and sense of, 194
self-help programs, online, 231
self-judgment, self-compassion *vs.*, 63
self-portrait, best, making, 199–200
self-realization, 8
self-reflection, feedback and, 223
self-regulation, 14*t*
self-statements
    negative, 49*t*
    positive, 48, 49*t*
self-worth
    finding, 166
    need for, 165
Seligman, M. E. P., xi, 1, 2, 3, 4, 19, 22,
    39, 72, 79, 111, 113, 116, 117, 119,
    120, 122, 127, 130, 156, 157, 159,
    190, 232
Seligman, N., 3, 4, 194
serenity, 46
shared rituals, developing, 110
shattered vase metaphor, trauma survi-
    vors and, 110–11
Sheldon, K. M., 9, 136
Shelton, C. M., 177

Shimai, S., 137
Simon, P., 18
sky at night story, 192–93
smartphone
    apps, 238–39
    PP interventions via, 225
smiling, 101
Smit, A., 227
Snyder, C. R., 158, 179, 180
social agents, 28, 238
social functioning, gratitude and, 175–76
social intelligence, 13t
social interactions, reflecting on, 132–33
social support
    health issues and lack of, 131
    perceived vs. received, 131–32
social well-being, 8
Social Well-Being Scale, 227
society, positive psychology and, 30–36
Socrates, 39
soft fascination, green color and, 51–52
soldier mental fitness, 22
solution-focused brief therapy, 20
solution-focused interviewing, 195, 203, 207
solution-focused leadership, 24–25

solution-focused organization, 24
solution-focused questions
    about hope, 183–84, 185
    asking, 185
solutions, thinking of, 223
somatic health services, online positive psychology interventions and, 233
SONG. see Seeking of Noetic Goals (SONG)
soothing system, 62–63
sparkling moments, reporting, 208
special moments, defining, 58
spirituality, 15t, 153, 159, 166, 190–93
    practicing, 191
    resilience and three Cs of, 191
sports, positive psychology and, 29–30
SQSS. see Strengths Q-sort Self-Assessment Scale (SQSS)
stable narratives, 83
Stam, P., 24
starfish story, positive difference in, 198
state gratitude, 169
Steen, T. A., 4
Stoics, 40
Strength Cards (Boniwell), 229
strength ears, listening with, 209–10
strength-perspective, 19–20
strength roadmap, creating, 17

strengths
  cards describing, 229–30
  celebrating, 34–35
  character, 8–18
  defining, 15
  diagnostics directed to, therapeutic
    value of, 226
  discovering, 20
  focusing on, ix, xi, 202–3
  growth mindset and, 220
  imagining a future with, 34
  potential *vs.* manifest, 15–16
  professional, searching for, 35
  student, development of, 25
  supervision and focus on, 208–9
  talents *vs.,* 15
  talking about, 16–17
  see also character strengths
strengths date, planning, 129
StrengthsFinder, 11, 15, 227
StrengthsFinder 2.0, 15
Strengths Q-sort Self-Assessment Scale
  (SQSS), 227–28
stretch goals, 180
students, focusing on strengths of,
  25
subgoals, 197
subjective well-being, 8

success
  celebrating, 206
  finding previous, 200
  five things to do for, 197
  focus on, 202–6
  goals and, 197
  identifying, 199
  interview about, 212
  maximizing, 210–11
  positive emotions and, 196
  Winnie-the-Pooh on, 204–5
  see also accomplishment
success box, making, 200–201
success certificate, creating, 206
successful memories, savoring, 205
successful people, goals and, 196–97
suicide
  character strengths and reducing risk
    of, 10
  despair and, 179
Super Better online game, 230
supervision
  focusing on strengths in, 208–9
  focusing on what is well done, 224
  positive, 195, 207–14
supporters, finding, 143
surprise task, 139
surprising someone, 138–39

survival-oriented behavior, negative
emotions and, 43
survivors of trauma
choosing role of victim or survivor,
105
reappraisal of life priorities and, 167
shattered vase metaphor and, 110–11
solution-focused questions for, 104
Susskind, L., 124
SWLS: Satisfaction With Life Scale, 227

take home ideas, asking about, 214
talent
grit vs., 216
growth mindset and, 220
identifying, 199
strength vs., 15
Tamir, M., 75, 76
Tan, S. A., 50
Tanaka-Matsumi, J., 137
Taoism, 30
taste of food, focus on, 55
teamwork, 13t
technology, positive psychology and,
27–28
Tedeschi, R. G., 102
temperance, character strengths related
to, 14t

10 million dollars lost anecdote, 203
ten-year plan, writing, 206
thankfulness
defined, 169
writing about, 61
see also gratitude
thank-you note, writing, 173–74
thank-you-therapy, 176
thought-action repertoires, positive emotions and, 43–44
three blessings exercise, 56
"three degrees of separation," happiness
in friendships and, 130
three funny things exercise, 56–57
thrivers, 104, 106
time, valuing, 54
"toward goals," athletes and, 30
training, 225
trait gratitude, 169
tranquility, imagery for, 68
transcendence, character strengths
encompassed in, 14t–15t, 62, 153,
166
trauma survivors. see survivors of trauma
traumatic experiences
gratitude in wake of, 177
talking about, 103
Trexles, L., 179

trust, mutual, 124
trust development, 124
trust repair, 124
Tugade, M. M, 236
two most important moments in life, 159

unexpected positive actions, 138
United Nations, constructive journalism and, 29
Uplifted online game, 230, 234
Uplift online game, 234
upward arrow technique, 114
useful things, focus on, 69

vacation planning, 94–95
Vaillant, G. E., 120
Vallerand, R. J., 215
values
    living in line with, 165
    need for, 164–65
van Woerkom, M., 22
Vella-Broderick, D., 232
VIA Inventory of Character Strengths, 129, 157, 199, 226–27
VIA Signature Strengths test, 11
victim
    choosing role of survivor or, 105–6
    seeing yourself as, 104

virtual reality, positive mood and, 27–28
virtues, classification of, 12*t*–15*t*
Vohs, K. D., 153, 162, 165
vulnerability, expressing, 62

Wansink, B., 136
wanting, liking *vs.*, 40–41
Warwick-Edinburgh Mental Well-Being Scale (WEMWBS), 227
water the flowers, not the weeds, 122
Watson, T., 203
weaknesses, mainstream psychology and, 8
Webb,T., 237
Weissman, A., 179
well-being, 19, 20, 21, 30, 75
    character strengths and, 9–10
    chronic pain and, 73
    components of, 8
    engagement and, 79
    gratitude and, 175–76
    hope and, 178, 180
    meaning and, 154, 158, 159
    mental health and, 2
    online positive psychology interventions and, 233
    performing acts of kindness and, 136
    personal growth and, 82

positive design and, 27
questionnaires for measuring, 227
religion and, 190–91
self-determination theory and, 11
spirituality and, 191
workplace, 22
see also happiness; health
well-being theory (Seligman), xi, 1
five pillars of, 6–7
see also accomplishment; engagement; meaning; positive emotions; relationships
WEMWBS. *see* Warwick-Edinburgh Mental Well-Being Scale (WEMWBS)
what-if game, playing, 107
what works well, focus on, 69
WHO. *see* World Health Organization
Wiethoff, C., 124
Winnie-the-Pooh on success, 204–5
wisdom, 12t, 231

Wiseman, R., 196
Wong, P. T. P., 158, 160, 161
work, ensuring connections at, 134–35
working on progress, in positive supervision, 207
workplace
enhancing hope in, 188
hope and performance in, 180
plants in, 25
positive conversations in, 205
positive psychology in, 21–25
World Health Organization (WHO), positive mental health described by, 2
worst-case scenario, imagining, 114
write, read, and burn, 108–9
Wu Wei, 55

Yardley, L., 237
"yes, and" *vs.* "yes, but," 147–48, 148t

zest, 13t

About the Author

Fredrike Bannink is a clinical psychologist and a Master of Dispute Resolution. She has a therapy, training, coaching, and mediation practice in Amsterdam, the Netherlands. Fredrike is a senior lecturer and supervisor at various postgraduate institutes and is also an internationally renowned keynote speaker, trainer, and author of more than thirty books.

Fredrike Bannink is a pioneer in recognizing, applying, and writing about the many possibilities of positive psychology. She is a member of the editorial board of two journals of positive psychology. Not surprisingly, her signature character strength is curiosity and interest in the world.

www.fredrikebannink.com